Counseling
Families

RESOURCES FOR
CHRISTIAN COUNSELING

RESOURCES FOR CHRISTIAN COUNSELING

1. Innovative Approaches to Counseling   *Gary R. Collins*

2. Counseling Christian Workers   *Louis McBurney*

3. Self-Talk, Imagery, and Prayer in Counseling
   H. Norman Wright

4. Counseling Those with Eating Disorders
   Raymond E. Vath

5. Counseling the Depressed   *Archibald D. Hart*

6. Counseling for Family Violence and Abuse
   Grant L. Martin

7. Counseling in Times of Crisis
   Judson J. Swihart and Gerald C. Richardson

8. Counseling and Guilt   *Earl D. Wilson*

9. Counseling and the Search for Meaning   *Paul R. Welter*

10. Counseling for Unplanned Pregnancy and Infertility
    Everett L. Worthington, Jr.

11. Counseling for Problems of Self-Control
    Richard P. Walters

12. Counseling for Substance Abuse and Addiction
    Stephen Van Cleave, Walter Byrd, Kathy Revell

13. Counseling and Self-Esteem   *David E. Carlson*

14. Counseling Families   *George A. Rekers*

15. Counseling and Homosexuality   *Earl D. Wilson*

(Other volumes forthcoming)

VOLUME FOURTEEN

Counseling Families

GEORGE A. REKERS, Ph.D.

RESOURCES FOR
CHRISTIAN COUNSELING

—————— General Editor ——————

Gary R. Collins, Ph.D.

WORD BOOKS
PUBLISHER
WACO, TEXAS
A DIVISION OF
WORD, INCORPORATED

Unless indicated otherwise, Scripture quotations in this volume are from the New International Version of the Bible, © 1983 by the New York International Bible Society. Used by permission of Zondervan Bible Publishers. Those identified NASB are from the New American Standard Bible, © The Lockman Foundation 1960, 1962, 1963, 1968, 1971, 1972, 1975, 1977. Used by permission. Those identified TLB are from The Living Bible, © 1971 Tyndale House Publishers, Wheaton, Ill.; used by permission.

Library of Congress Cataloging-in-Publication Data

Rekers, George Alan.
    Counseling families / George A. Rekers.
        p.   cm. — (Resources for Christian counseling ; v. 14)
    Bibliography: p.
    Includes index.
    ISBN 0-8499-0595-8 :
    1. Church work with families.   2. Family—Religious life.
3. Family—Pastoral counseling of. I. Title. II. Series.
BV4438.R45   1988
253.5—dc19   87-35392
                                                  CIP

89801239 FG 987654321

Printed in the United States of America

CONTENTS

EDITOR'S PREFACE

Almost every week my mailbox contains at least one or two
letters inviting me to attend or speak at another conference on
the family. Academic institutions, professional societies, Christian organizations, and especially church groups seem to be
sponsoring an endless stream of seminars, workshops, weekend
retreats, and banquets that focus on family issues.

Military leaders have discovered that family instability
and frequent separations can distract service personnel and
interfere with combat readiness. Innumerable government
programs have been created in an effort to deal with family-
related domestic issues and even the business community has
come to recognize that family problems can undermine em-
ployee effectiveness, decrease morale, and indirectly sheer
corporate profits. James Dobson's popular Focus on the Family films and daily radio programs continue to attract a wide
audience, and a variety of magazine articles all reinforce the

7

same message: the modern family is beset with problems and in need of help.

Several years ago, over two thousand Christian leaders met for a week-long Congress on the Family that attempted to analyze and suggest ways to solve some of our most pressing family problems. Participants attended simultaneous sessions led by some of the best-known and most qualified family-life experts in North America. At the end of our time together, we published a carefully written, biblically based "affirmation on the family" and went forth determined to improve family life in our homes, churches, and communities.

But I wonder if things are any better. In spite of all this activity, marital problems still are common, the divorce rate is high, and family unity appears to be rare. Counselors continue to work with dysfunctional families and pastors repeatedly discover that the homes of some of the most prominent church members are torn by strife and discord. Even family counselors and Christian leaders themselves often face tension, communication breakdowns, and interpersonal problems when they come home from their counseling offices and other places of ministry.

In planning the Resources for Christian Counseling series of books, my colleagues at Word, Inc. agreed that we would need a solid volume on family counseling to be written by a competent author who was both well-qualified and highly experienced as a family counselor. Dr. George A. Rekers is such a man and this book will surely be of great practical help to those Christians who counsel with families.

Each of the books in this counseling series is intended to be practical and helpful. Written by counseling experts, each of whom has a strong Christian commitment and extensive counseling experience, the volumes are intended to be examples of accurate psychology and careful use of Scripture. Each is intended to have a clear evangelical perspective, careful documentation, a strong practical orientation, and freedom from the sweeping statements and undocumented rhetoric that sometimes characterize books in the counseling field. Our goal is to provide books that are clearly written, useful, up-to-date overviews of the issues faced by contemporary Christian counselors. All of the Resources for Christian Counseling books have similar bindings and together they will comprise a helpful encyclopedia of Christian counseling.

I first met the author of this book in the summer of 1984 at the Shoreham Hotel in Washington, D.C. Along with Dr. Judson Swihart (who has also authored a volume in this series), George Rekers was coordinator of the National Leadership Forum on Family Well-Being. This was a "think-tank" meeting, attended by academic, theological, counseling, and government people. We met, not to bemoan the fate of the family, but to ponder what could be done, in practical ways, to strengthen families (especially Christian families) and to help them become more stable. Later, George Rekers combined all of the formal conference papers and discussion summaries into an impressive book on family life. (Edited by George Rekers and published by Regal, the book is entitled *Family Building: Six Qualities of a Strong Family*.) This book was one of several that the author has written as the result of his continuing study of family issues.

George Rekers also continues to work as a family counselor. He teaches full time on the faculty of a prestigious medical school in the South, works as a writer and researcher, and frequently travels overseas to conduct workshops and training sessions. Most often these overseas classes relate to family issues and frequently they involve audiences of missionaries, theological students, and local church leaders. Whenever possible, the whole Rekers family goes on these trips. George is *not* a man who ignores his own wife and children while he runs around the world lecturing about family togetherness!

In reading the following pages you will meet a family man and a first-rate professional helper who has a deep understanding of family issues and an impressive knowledge of the Bible. The author's conclusions are practical, illustrated frequently with examples from his own counseling experiences, clearly documented by scientific research, and presented with a warmth and sensitivity that makes the book a pleasure to read.

This will not be the last book on family counseling. The family conferences, seminars, and workshops will continue to be held and family members will continue to have problems. But when these families are in your church or when they bring their problems to your counseling office, this book should be a helpful guide as you work in one of the most challenging areas of Christian service: counseling families.

Gary R. Collins, Ph.D.
Kildeer, Illinois

INTRODUCTION

THE EXCRUCIATINGLY BRIGHT KLIEG LIGHTS glared in my eyes from several directions as I was escorted to my assigned seat in a stately formal hearing room of the United States Senate. The Senate aide asked me to sit in the front row facing the senators, and I could barely hear over the myriad of conversations in the room as he introduced me to the man seated to my immediate right, Dr. George Gallup of the Gallup Poll. The television cameras were aimed in our direction as Dr. Gallup and I were awaiting the start of the hearings before the Senate Subcommittee on Family and Human Services. There was no doubt about it, they were anticipating the release of the findings of a new Gallup Poll. George Gallup and I were both taking a few last moments to review our notes for our oral testimony. Somehow, he seemed more relaxed than I, appearing to be oblivious to the cameras.

While cameras flashed and the TV crew focused on him, he reviewed the findings of a number of Gallup polls taken over recent decades. He forcefully concluded that the American people's desire for a fulfilling family life is as strong now as it was fifty years ago but that the contemporary challenge is that diminishing numbers in our country are putting their family values into practice.

In light of the largely unrelenting divorce rate, which disrupts approximately one out of every two marriages in the United States, the senators had scheduled this hearing on "the broken family." My own testimony focused on the effects of divorce on children's emotional, social, and academic well-being.[1] A number of the expert witnesses that same day described other aspects of the economic and psychological impact of divorce upon individuals, communities, and our nation.

What can the church do to minister to families who are struggling to fulfill the desire for a stable family life? In recent decades, pastors have increasingly been called upon to counsel families in distress. Hundreds of Christian counseling centers have been established within and alongside the church in our local communities. Family counseling is in great demand, and there is no sign that this demand will diminish in the closing years of the twentieth century and the first decades of the twenty-first century. Increasingly, pastors with limited formal Bible college or seminary training in the field of family counseling are being called upon to offer guidance to families in their churches. In fact, a recent survey found that 77 percent of people in a community preferred clergy counseling for family problems compared to 14 percent who preferred nonreligious family counseling. For no other problem (depression, severe mental illness, etc.) did such a high percentage of respondents prefer religious counseling.[2]

To many pastors, it seems quite appropriate to respond to such a need by providing counseling services, because after all, the family was the first social institution created by God and it remains his chosen environment for bringing children into the world and for nurturing and discipling them. The very fabric of both the church and society is torn as families disintegrate. How could the pastor and the church possibly stand by silently and allow suffering families to disintegrate before their eyes, especially in view of the urgent cries for help?

I worked as a clinical psychologist for several years in a family counseling center in Van Nuys, California. This Christian counseling center had been started by one local church but became an independent service sponsored by several evangelical churches. It employed about twelve part-time and full-time staff counselors who worked together with pastors involved in counseling individuals and families. For more than a dozen years, I've met with pastors in groups or individually discussing counseling needs of families in their congregations and community. The pastors usually set the agenda in these meetings, sometimes presenting cases saying, "Let me describe a family I'm counseling." Then we ponder counseling techniques and theological principles, which always results in a mutually rewarding interchange. One theme of these discussions has been the increase of family problems both in the community and in the church.

In 1950, only one in twelve children in America lived in a single-parent home. But as a result of the increased divorce rate and the fourfold increase in the number of unwed mothers, approximately one of every four children in the United States currently lives in a single-parent home, and fully half of all children living today will spend a portion of their childhood years in a single-parent home. The U.S. Census Bureau forecasts that fully two-thirds of all children born in 1985 will spend at least a portion of their childhood years in a single-parent family.[3] The by-product of a pervasive lack of enduring commitment is the tragic emotional suffering of children of divorce.

In his chapter in the book *Family Building*, which I edited, Dr. Armand Nicholi, a psychiatrist at Harvard University, focused on the research finding that parents in the United States "spend less time with their children than in any other nation in the world, perhaps with the exception of England—the one country that surpasses the United States in violent crime and juvenile delinquency."[4] Too often, careerism and materialism

13

have competed with commitment to family, with children suffering as the unfortunate victims. Many of our citizens both within and outside the church have uncritically accepted divorce for any and every reason. Children and teenagers in so many of our homes are exposed to massive doses of television programing which conveys distorted values regarding family relationships. In school, in the workplace, and in the neighborhood, family members are exposed to unbiblical attitudes regarding family life, and if these values are not reasonably challenged, the family may accept them and experience an erosion of their own family bonds.[5] In this environment, it has become an urgent necessity for pastors and other Christians involved in counseling to become equipped to use the tools of family counseling.

Although I have specifically addressed the needs of families in my own home country, the United States, I am fully aware of the parallel needs in many other countries of the world. I was reminded of this fact only this morning as I taught a class in counseling at the Tyndale Theological Seminary in Badhoevedorp, Holland. Even as I write these words, just outside of Amsterdam, I am thinking of the faces of my counseling students from Africa, Asia, various European countries as well as from the Americas. Human needs vary from nation to nation around the world, but it seems to be a mark of the late twentieth century that problems in living are increasingly manifested in that most intimate set of human relationships, the family.

Just a few years ago, I was invited to speak to the semiannual field conference of an evangelical missionary organization with workers in Austria, Greece, and Turkey (among other countries). At this ten-day workshop just outside of Vienna, Austria, I was asked many questions about how to counsel European families. Many of the issues were the same as those in the United States, even though the cultural setting and traditions differ significantly from locality to locality. The American missionaries in these rather unevangelized countries found that one of their key opportunities for reaching others with the gospel was in the area of providing family counseling. The needs loom so great and the suffering penetrates so pervasively that Christians equipped to counsel families often find receptive ears to the gospel message.

My experiences as a visiting lecturer in Europe and my students from Third World countries at U.S. universities have convinced me that many of the needs of pastors are the same the world around. It is a wise Christian worker who responds to the need for family counseling.

In these pages, I have used numerous case studies to illustrate the truth of what is written. All of the stories are based upon real cases; however, names and details have been altered to protect confidentiality. The charts and lists in this book are designed to aid you, the counselor, in the practical application of more effective family counseling. The counselor is permitted to make copies of any chart for himself or herself for use in counseling sessions.

I gratefully acknowledge the diligent and accurate word processing of various drafts of this book by Becky Kilgus. I also thank Dr. Gary Collins, general editor of this book series, and Carey Moore, my editor at Word, Inc., for expert and wise guidance. In the midst of this demanding project, I received some special encouragement from Willi Grander, a visiting medical student I sponsored from the University of Innsbruck, Austria. Thank you, Willi, for the invaluable gift of mutual friendship. Finally, I enthusiastically acknowledge my wonderful wife Sharon and our five fantastic sons for all their loving support and patience while I penned this work. I would like to say that any errors in this book are the fault of the numerous interruptions by my energetic children, but that would be neither fair nor true; in fact, my family has taught me at least as much as my mentors, my textbooks, and my counseling clients, and, alas, I must personally take responsibility for any manuscript errors my readers are kind enough to point out to me.

Counseling
Families

RESOURCES FOR
CHRISTIAN COUNSELING

CHAPTER ONE

THE NEED FOR FAMILY COUNSELING

"HECTIC" BEST DESCRIBED the unrelenting pace of Pastor Andrew Morgan's schedule that day. After his early morning devotions and completion of his Bible lesson for the evening prayer meeting, he dashed off to the municipal hospital to visit three recuperating surgery patients and one new mother. Then driving to the other end of town, he met the church youth minister over lunch to finalize the summer calendar of activities. By the time he returned to his office, five phone messages had accumulated, but he had time to return only two of the most urgent before a young couple arrived for their 2:00 P.M. premarital counseling session. That lasted longer than he had planned, so it was 3:30 P.M. before he could return the other urgent call. A single-parent mother was calling to tell him about her overdue rent and her discouragement and to request that the church pray for her son's severe behavior problems. After signing some correspondence and asking the church secretary to have the benevolence fund treasurer contact the single parent, Pastor Morgan hurried home for dinner so he could get back for Wednesday evening services. After arriving home with his family and helping the preschoolers get to bed, he collapsed on the sofa, just as the phone rang again. His wife sweetly called to him from the kitchen, "It's for you, dear. It's Mrs. Darnell."

"It's my fifteen-year-old, Shawn," Mrs. Darnell stuttered as she wept. "After an argument with my husband, he ran to his room and slammed the door. We waited for him to cool down. But when he didn't come out again later, we knocked on his door and then opened it. He was gone, and we found a note saying he has run away and not to call the police because he has his hunting gun and he'll kill himself if the police come after him."

After calmly helping Mrs. Darnell to think through the most logical places to find Shawn and praying with her over the phone, Pastor Morgan recommended, "Follow through now on what we talked about, and after you find Shawn call me. I'll schedule a time to meet your family in my office or in your home."

The next morning, Mrs. Darnell called just after 9:00 A.M. "I called Mrs. Lloyd and she told me Shawn was there with her family. He stayed there overnight and agreed to meet with you if his dad also comes. You know how little time Tom spends with the two boys. He always spends long hours at his business, and no matter what I say, he never comes home earlier. The boys need their dad's attention, but practically the only time he talks to them is when he's yelling at them to do their homework or something else. The blowup last night was over Tom's grounding Shawn for the rest of the semester for getting a poor progress report from school."

Pastor Morgan met with the family late that afternoon in his office. He encouraged family members to describe their present conflict, their feelings, and their hopes for improved relationships. When he shared some Scripture on forgiveness, Tom shocked the rest of the family by asking Shawn to forgive him for dishing out punishment in anger. Pastor Morgan negotiated a new agreement in which Shawn's privileges for going out with friends were to be determined daily depending on his completion of homework on the previous day. Although this seemed to resolve the present crisis, Pastor Morgan knew that the underlying family problems needed attention. He agreed to see them for ongoing family counseling on the condition that Shawn be evaluated further by a Christian psychologist for his depression and suicide potential.

FAMILY PROBLEMS BROUGHT TO PASTORS

Since the early 1980s, the National Association of Evangelicals (N.A.E.) has had an ongoing Task Force on the Family with representatives from each member denominational group. In addition, a number of family specialists have been invited to join the task force, and I have been serving in this capacity. The task force has been meeting regularly to promote the strengthening of families through the work of the local church. We designed a survey which was administered to a sample of 337 pastors asking them about their counseling with families. The results were released at the 1985 N.A.E. annual convention by Professor Ted Ward of Michigan State University and Trinity Evangelical Divinity School.

One section on this survey asked pastors to list the topics for which they most needed family ministry resources. Overwhelmingly they wanted resources on two family topics: *communication skills* and *financial affairs*. Other frequently listed topics, in decreasing order of priority, were:

>parent/adolescent relationships,
>child-rearing,
>marital and premarital counseling, and
>alcoholism and drug abuse.

These were the six topics on which pastors most desired resources to assist their work in helping families.

This study had a number of other findings. The pastors generally believed that the problems of Christian families were becoming more and more similar to the problems of non-Christian families over the years of their ministry. When asked, "Who brings requests to you for help on family problems?" the pastors reported that women brought far more requests for help to them than men; and married couples also came in for help more frequently than men alone. Secular counselors similarly find that while more teenage boys are referred for adjustment problems than girls, more adult women come for help than men, so that psychologists and psychiatrists specializing in dealing with adults see primarily women in American culture. This is evidently not because women have more problems than men but because women are more willing to label something as a problem, admit it's a problem, and then seek help for it. For family counseling, women very often make the first contact.

The pastors surveyed were also asked to list in order the leading family problems brought to their attention. The four most frequent family problems were

1. communication problems,
2. financial problems,
3. emotional problems, and
4. poor relationships with children.

These problems, in terms of frequency of occurrence, are not unlike those reported by secular counselors, except that a substantially lower percentage of the pastors were reporting infidelity problems; secular counselors rate unfaithfulness as one of the most frequent problems that they see.

Fifty-eight percent of the pastors surveyed agreed with this statement: "Family breakdown is becoming a more common problem in my congregation." However, almost half of the pastors surveyed never or only once attended any kind of workshop or program that dealt with gaining skills in family counseling or family ministry. Half of the pastors indicated that they had never turned to another pastor for help with family problems in their congregation, and almost half said that they had never helped another pastor in such matters. At the same time, in the comment section of this survey, the pastors indicated distrust of counselors outside the church or outside the Christian faith. On the other hand, most of the pastors felt that they were skilled in dealing with the family problems that came up in their church.

TWENTIETH-CENTURY CHANGES IN FAMILY LIFE

In recent decades, many pastors and other Christian counselors have found themselves spending more and more of their time in family counseling. What is it about the state of the family today that has led to the increasing demand for family counseling?

This was one of the issues that surfaced when the National Leadership Forum on Family Well-Being was convened in June 1984 to explore ways of strengthening family life in America. One of the major speakers to address this forum was psychiatrist Armand Nicholi. Dr. Nicholi spoke in one of the expansive ballrooms in the old and elegant Shoreham Hotel in Washington, D.C., the historic site of the inaugural balls for United States presidents. He provided a sobering assessment of American family life.

In any nation, children and youth reflect in large measure the state of families in that society. If we look at our nation's children and adolescents today, we observe certain trends that tell us something about what is happening to the families in this country.

Among children and adolescents is a marked increase in suicide which concerns all of us. We also note an increase in violent crime perpetrated on children and perpetrated by them. We can't help but be concerned with the increase in emotional disturbance, in depression, in sexual identity problems (homosexuality appears to be on the increase). Furthermore, we observe a phenomenon unique in our history, namely the epidemic of drugs: the tendency to inhale, ingest or inject into the human body a number of psychoactive substances to alter the emotional state of the individual.

Now when we look at these trends in children, we notice that they parallel trends occurring in the family—certain changes that began some thirty years ago.

What are these changes?

1. The care of the children relegated to others.
2. An increase of mothers working outside the home.
3. An accelerated divorce rate.[1]

Nicholi pointed out that parents have increasingly been relegating the care of their children to baby-sitters, day-care centers, and nurseries. He noted that the television set has become a pervasive influence in America and in many other countries in the world, conveying many antifamily values to children.

Divorce and Illegitimacy

There are many ironies that occur in Western societies today. On the one hand, increasing numbers of unmarried couples are living together, and many young adults are postponing marriage to a later age; but on the other hand, at the same time nearly half of all marriages, when they do eventually occur, end in divorce. Similarly, since the 1960s there has been widespread use of contraceptives in the nations of the Western world, yet the rate of illegitimacy has doubled in the past thirty years and the percentage of pregnancies ended by abortion has been rapidly increasing.

In the United States from 1970 to 1982, the number of children living with a never-married mother increased more than fourfold from .5 to 2.8 million. Currently, about one of every five children is born out of wedlock. The number of children living with a divorced mother more than doubled from 1970 to 1982 from 2.3 to 5.1 million. Another 3.1 million children live with separated mothers.[2]

The rate of growth in the number of single-parent families is approximately twenty times the rate of growth in the number of two-parent families. Divorce is the largest contributor to new cases of poverty. Fifty-two percent of the female-headed households in the country, involving six million children, are living in poverty.[3] Overall, the divorce rate has increased several hundred percent since 1890 even though the rate has dropped slightly in the 1980s.[4]

Parental Inaccessibility

But it is not only divorce which contributes to parental inaccessibility in our society, because fully 52 percent of married couples with children have both partners working outside the home, often overcommitted to careers in terms of time spent away from their children. As a consequence, there are currently six and a half million children under age twelve who are "latchkey children"—that is, children who are left unattended for extended periods of most days.[5]

The increased number of dual career families in combination with overcommitment to work has led to the situation in the United States in which parents, on the average, spend less time with their children than in any other nation in the world, with the possible exception of England. Nicholi contends that this factor alone has been responsible for much of the increased emotional problems of children and youth in our families today. ". . . if people with severe emotional nonorganic disorders have anything in common, it's that they have experienced, sometime in their childhood, an absence of an accessible parent because of death, divorce or a time-demanding job."[6]

Some radical elements of the women's movement have contributed to the confusion of many women in our society. They feel somehow that if they're submissive to their husbands' desires and become full-time homemakers, they're not really equal, but they're not comfortable with the "liberated" lifestyle either.

Mothers of young children are also pressured into the work force by our society's emphasis on money. Many women are uncomfortable if they're out working in a career full-time because they feel guilty about not spending enough time with the children. But they'd feel guilty if they stayed home, too, because they feel that they're something less than productive members of society if they're not bringing in a paycheck. So, a woman who cares for children as a paid day-care worker at a day-care center feels better about herself (with her professional title and paycheck) than the mother who takes care of her own children at home. What if the mother has a college degree and she's not earning a salary with it? Well, many people will tell her that she's wasting her education. Such is our materialistic culture: If you can attach a dollar sign to something, then it has value. The fact that a mother uses her trained intellect and education to care for her own children doesn't seem to carry much water in a society that measures value in dollars and titles.

Many parents prefer to talk about quality rather than quantity of time with their children. They assume, "If we have good quality time that will make up for lack of quantity." Books on the best-seller lists have discussed the "one-minute father," the "one-minute mother," and they promote little phrases like the "quality phone call." But time with your child is like oxygen in the air we breathe.[7]

Certainly we need good quality air to survive. If the air where you are sitting were polluted with excessive carbon monoxide or soot, you would suffer health problems, but it's not only the quality of the air that is important, it's the quantity. We can't survive with just a little bit of high quality air from 8:00 A.M. to 8:15 A.M. and expect to be able to do without any at 9:00 A.M. So, "time with children is like oxygen." They need good quality, but they need the quantity as well.

COMMON ROOTS OF MANY FAMILY PROBLEMS

Many other problems experienced by children and youth result from the deteriorating conditions in family life. For example, the Center for Child Abuse and Neglect estimates that at least 1.3 million cases of abuse and neglect occur each year in American families. Sixty thousand juvenile prostitutes are reported annually in the United States, and it appears that 80 percent of these are runaways. Each year 1.8 million young people run away from home and 10 percent of those who return home report that they were sexually exploited while they were missing.[8]

Research studies indicate that adolescent girls whose fathers are separated from them due to divorce are at a much higher likelihood of becoming pregnant in their teen years.[9] Boys who live in a single-parent home created by divorce have exceedingly higher rates of behavior problems, emotional disturbances, poor self-esteem, social immaturity, sexual identity problems, drug and alcohol abuse, delinquent behavior, suicide, school adjustment problems, and academic problems than children from two-parent families.[10]

The instability of family life in recent decades has been responsible for the increased demand for Christian family counseling. The presenting problems which lead to the request for family counseling can be varied: child behavior problems, alcohol or drug abuse by a family member, parent-child adjustment to a remarriage, pregnancy in an unwed teenager, communication problems in the family, coping with unemployment, child custody disputes, severe emotional disturbance in a family member, delinquency problems, refusal to complete homework assignments, teenage rebellion, child discipline problems, peer pressures, and so forth.

I recently attended the Annual Conference of the Family Research Council held at George Washington University in Washington, D.C., where Dr. Peter Uhlenberg, a professor of sociology at the University of North Carolina at Chapel Hill, spoke on the recent changes in the well-being of adolescents in American society.[11] Uhlenberg reminded us that most of the social indicators that social scientists and policy makers thought were essential for the well-being of children were moving in the direction that should have resulted in improvement of adolescent well-being. However, the research documents that the well-being of teenagers has actually declined in this same time period. It had been widely assumed that poverty, large family size and low parental education were negative influences on child development. In the last twenty-five years, the proportion of teenagers who lived in homes without these three characteristics (poverty, large family size and undereducated parents) doubled from one-third to approximately two-thirds. At the same time, school systems increased expenditures per pupil, the qualifications of teachers increased, and the size of classes decreased. Large increases were made in social welfare expenditures for children and youth by the federal government, and hundreds of new programs were funded and administered by numerous federal agencies. However, the measures of well-being for adolescents have actually declined over this same time period:

• School achievement and intellectual performance have declined.

• As the death rate in the U.S. population has declined by over 23 percent from 1960 to 1980, there has been a decline in death rate for every age group except those age fifteen to twenty-four years. Death rates in this group from motor vehicle accidents, suicide, and homicide have increased dramatically.

• The juvenile delinquency rate increased between 1960 and 1980.

• Drug and alcohol abuse markedly increased.

• The proportion of teenagers reporting having had sexual intercourse doubled between 1971 and 1979 leading (1) to a rapid increase in the proportion of all children born to unwed teenage mothers, (2) to increased numbers of teenagers contracting sexually transmitted diseases, and (3) to a marked increase in numbers of abortions performed on teenagers.

If our nation's children are increasingly living with more material resources, in smaller families with more higher educated parents, why has there been such a substantial decline in the well-being of teenagers? Uhlenberg contends that the most critical determinant of child and youth well-being is the bond between child and parent. He argues that the deterioration in the quantity and quality of parent-child relationships since 1960 has been associated with two social trends—(1) the increase in the female labor force participation and (2) the increase in the divorce rate. Both of these factors have a direct consequence for the relationship between parents and children. Uhlenberg points to the research finding that "quality time" of mothers with their children is quite limited when mothers work outside the home. In addition, significant emotional upheaval is experienced by children whose parents divorce.

The declining commitment of parents to children has been associated with an increase in the commitment of adults to their own individual self-fulfillment. "The pursuit of self-fulfillment, or self-actualization, or self-realization necessarily implies a reduction in self-sacrificing behavior. In such an environment, children fare badly. The needs of immature and dependent children are not going to be met satisfactorily in a society where adults are unwilling to sacrifice their personal goals for their children's welfare."[12]

In a study of changed attitudes in the 1970s, Dr. Daniel Yankelovich summarized his research with the statement that today's parents expect to make fewer sacrifices for their children than in the past.[13] Uhlenberg's critique of American culture points to a move away from the Judeo-Christian values of community and self-sacrifice for the welfare of others toward a more selfish individualism which is inconsistent with strong families and strong communities. At the same time, the media's impact on our culture has increased, with both programing and advertising repeatedly suggesting that materialism is the route to personal happiness and that personal happiness is the highest goal we should seek.

Many of the problems that will confront the family counselor are a by-product of the fact that increasing numbers of individuals no longer view husband-wife and parent-child relationships as permanent. Problems are increasingly experienced in the earlier stages of the life span, because more and more parents have been shying away from their responsibility of caring for children. At the same time, more and more adult children have been shying away from their responsibility of caring for their elderly parents. To the extent that our culture has increasingly set aside God's laws for family life, we have seen an abandonment of the continuity and commitment that hold the family together. The weak and dependent members of the family, both young and old, have suffered the greatest not only with regard to neglect, but with regard to the current advocacy for and practice of abortion, infanticide, and euthanasia, practices which were unthinkable only a few decades ago.[14]

A Focus for Family Counseling

We recognize the growing need for family counseling whether we look at the statistics of what's happening to many families in Western culture or whether we look at the survey data of pastors in evangelical churches. In light of these trends, what can Christian family counselors affirm regarding how families should and can function?

Every Christian counselor should have in mind a number of positive biblical teachings on the family. Frankly, family counseling is a very value-laden activity. For example, family counselors value good, clear, and open communication in a family as opposed to poor communication. Reconciliation of family members and resolution of conflicts are valued over and above the perpetuation of unresolved conflict. The active involvement of parents in child-rearing and in child care is valued instead of the neglect of children's needs.

The family coming to a pastor or Christian counselor will expect to experience counseling guided by Christian values regarding the family rather than the value systems that would be adopted by the secularistic counselor. Sometimes these values need to be explicitly stated by the family counselor, but in all cases they need to be implicitly followed.

How Did the Family Originate?

The expectations that one has for a family depend upon whether the family is recognized as a divinely created institution or considered a mere human invention of convenience. The secular family counselor assumes that the family is merely a human contract or social convention. In the latter case, there is no concept that family members have an accountability to God their Creator. The decision whether to have children or be deliberately childless is seen as merely a right of individuals to make their own choices. If marital conflict over such an issue escalates and persists, then abandonment of the family relationship is viewed as a viable option. However, these views are contrary to Scripture (Hebrews 13:4; 2 Corinthians 6:14; Ephesians 5:21–33; Psalm 127:1; Proverbs 18:22).[15]

By contrast, the Christian family counselor affirms the biblical teaching that God himself created the institution of the family when he created Eve for Adam and joined them in the lifelong covenant of marriage which included three parties: God, man, and woman (Genesis 2:22–24; Isaiah 49:15). When God created the family unit, it was intended in some sense to reflect his own image on the earth and he gave the command to be fruitful and multiply (Ephesians 5:22, 23; Genesis 1:27, 28).

How Are Family Relationships Defined?

Some secular family counselors use a highly flexible if not illogical definition of family relationships when referring to any individuals sharing the same household and economic resources as a "family" even though the individuals are unrelated to one another or may even be homosexual partners.

In contrast, the biblical definition of a family, recognized by the Christian counselor, is based on the nuclear family of a heterosexual married couple with their natural or adopted children. It also includes the family branches including all the nuclear families that are descended from a common ancestor.[16] In biblical terms, a family relationship between two individuals is created by heterosexual marriage, blood relationships to biological children and/or by formal adoption. The Christian family counselor would also recognize unadopted stepchildren and foster children as members of a family unit.

In contemporary society, with its confusion regarding what is a family and what is not a family, it is often important for the family counselor to clarify the commitments that underlie genuine family relationships and to distinguish these kinds of committed relationships from other kinds of human relationships. For example, an adopted child should be treated with the same level of commitment as a biological child, but a foster child represents a different level of commitment because the social agency may terminate the relationship by placing that child in another home. Furthermore, one's legal parental responsibility and authority over a foster child is somewhat different than that with a biological or adopted child. Sometimes the Christian counselor must emphasize how the biblical perspective differs from that of secular society. The Bible does not treat homosexual relationships as though they represented a "marriage" or a "family," regardless of how the individuals happen to feel about their relationship.

What Is the Purpose of the Family?

Some secular family counselors view the family rather exclusively in terms of the needs of the individual members of the family unit. They view optimal family functioning as the state in which the individual needs of individual family members are fulfilled at some reasonable level (even though some compromises might be involved). A family may view their home as merely a "filling station" where various family members drop by to have their needs "serviced." A person with this view might come to the conclusion, "If my needs can be better serviced outside my family, why shouldn't I go ahead and pursue different relationships?" The children's needs might be "serviced" by extensive use of day-care facilities rather than by parental supervision. Many of the functions of the family may be transferred to social agencies outside the family. In this view, even sexual needs could be gratified elsewhere if both husband and wife agree to an "open marriage." These are considered simply as "options" that people have.

By contrast, the Christian family counselor affirms that God has specific mandates for the family and for the individual roles within a family. The central purpose of the family is to glorify God and to advance his Kingdom. The Scripture teaches that this may be accomplished by having children if God so provides and discipling them to follow Christ. Ministries of hospitality, mercy, and evangelism are also integral parts of Christian family life.

The Bible describes children as a heritage from the Lord and a sacred trust given by God and placed into the parents' hands (Psalm 127, 128). Parents are therefore divine stewards who have received their responsibilities from God. This means they do not have the option of wholesale delegating or setting aside these responsibilities. Though the Christian family may wisely use other resources to fulfill its responsibility, the parents are personally urged not to exasperate their children but to bring the children up in the discipline and instruction of the Lord (Ephesians 6:4).

The Christian family counselor therefore cannot view parental inaccessibility as merely a socially acceptable "option" to be employed at the discretion of the individual parent. Instead, there are normative guidelines and commands from God himself which should govern family life and form the model family relationships (Genesis 33:5; Psalm 78:1–8; Deuteronomy 4:9; 6:1–9; 1 Timothy 2:15; Proverbs 17:6; Ephesians 6:1–4). Because the family has a divinely mandated set of functions and purposes, the Christian family counselor keeps these in mind as counseling goals. At many points in counseling, these goals need to be explicitly verbalized as the counselor is used by the Holy Spirit to guide the family into all truth.

For this reason, the Christian family counselor cannot endorse the practice of family members individually pursuing their own independent goals at the expense of total family needs. The family counselor needs to open Scripture and share God's basic plan which includes his design that families be productive for his Kingdom and that families identify their unique purpose on earth to fulfill God's plan (Genesis 1:27, 28; Matthew 28:18–20; Deuteronomy 6:7; 11:19; 1 Timothy 2:15–3:13; 1 Corinthians 7:2–16).

In setting goals for counseling sessions, the family counselor needs to call the family to the considerations of God's will for their lives with one another.

The counselor should point families to the explicit biblical commands regarding providing for children, providing for the physical needs of young and old dependent family members, caring for incapacitated family members, and extending help to the needy of one's community through family hospitality and acts of mercy.[17]

In conclusion, there is a growing need for family counseling because of the growth in the divorce rate, the increase in unmarried parenthood, the high level of sexual promiscuity, and the decline of parental responsibility for child-rearing. These practices decrease parental accessibility and weaken the parent-child bond. Therefore, pastors and other Christian counselors need to be particularly skilled in family counseling interventions. Positive affirmations regarding God's design for the family should provide the framework within which all family counseling proceeds.

CHAPTER TWO

DETECTING THE UNDERLYING PROBLEMS

ONE AFTERNOON, I received a phone call from the mother of a teenage girl, Malinda. She and her husband wanted to come in for counseling with Malinda because the girl was pregnant and unmarried. The mother was afraid her daughter was considering abortion and, as Christians, the parents found this totally unacceptable. That was the presenting problem. But that might not be the underlying problem. What might be the problems that underlie this surface problem? There are a number of possibilities.

Perhaps there is emotional distance between the father and this daughter. Research has indicated that unwed teenage girls are more likely to become pregnant where there is a distant relationship with the father.

Or perhaps Malinda has poor communication with her mother. Other studies have found that teenage girls who have good communication with their mothers have a much lower rate of pregnancy.

It could be that the pregnancy is due to incest, perhaps with the father or a brother. Incestuous relationships are four to five times more common in families with a stepfather than in families with a biological father present. We have a high frequency of stepfamilies due to the divorce and remarriage rates, so this could be an underlying problem.

Or perhaps the teenage girl is struggling with her parents for independence. Perhaps the parents have not been allowing her a normal, healthy type of independence, and she is reacting, in part, by trying to liberate herself and achieve adulthood by having a baby.

There are certainly other possibilities as well. So, we see how a surface problem presented to a family counselor might stem from any number of underlying problems. An obvious contributing problem here is a sin problem because Malinda had been sexually involved before marriage, either by choice (her sin) or by coercion (the rapist's sin). There are some families where the parents have never talked to their daughter about what is right and what is wrong sexually; therefore, lack of specific moral teaching could also be an underlying issue.

THE FIRST FAMILY COUNSELING SESSION

Typically a family member, such as Malinda's mother, calls the counselor requesting an appointment for help with a personal problem or, as was the case here, for assistance with a problem with another family member. Often the complaint is stated in terms of one particular family member ("Malinda is pregnant and considering an abortion," or, "My teenage son has been refusing to come home at our curfew time on school nights").

Many family counselors interpret such a complaint as merely meaning, "Ouch! My family is hurting."[1] Consequently, they request that all family members living in the household come in together for the first family counseling session. This provides an opportunity to gather firsthand information about how the family operates and what strategies family members use to cope with stress (in this case the stress of the initial counseling session).

The well-known family therapist Virginia Satir, on the other hand, usually insists on meeting with the husband and wife first for at least two counseling sessions without the children, in order to focus on their own relationship in addition to the difficulty they are experiencing as parents. If there are children under the age of four years, Satir might include them for some initial sessions, then work with the marital pair, and then include the young children again later in the family counseling process. Children over four are included in almost all of the family sessions, and this involves not only the child with the identified problem, but all the offspring living at home.[2] Other family counselors also see the parents first to orient them to the family therapy approach and then include all the children. Family therapist John E. Bell excludes children under the age of nine, believing that they have not developed in thinking ability enough to consider the family problems because they are still focused on their own self-centered feelings.[3]

Jay Haley, an influential author on family counseling, views the first family interview as the opportunity to negotiate with the family on what problem or problems need attention.[4] Through preplanned and systematic steps, Haley takes the family through interview stages intended (1) to get all family members to participate, (2) to have each family member identify the changes he or she wants, and (3) to define the family problem as completely as possible before making interventions.

"Experiential" family counselors begin in the first interview to press the family members to expose their vulnerabilities through self-disclosure. When family members complain to the counselor about one another, the counselor insists that they tell each person directly about their feelings. By forcing family members to talk to each other and disclose themselves, it is hoped that they will begin to untangle their family problems. Family therapist Walter Kempler uses this type of focus on the immediate process of family interaction in his more confronting approach to working with families.[5]

Different family counselors take different approaches to the initial family session, depending upon their theoretical orientation (see Appendix 1) and also depending upon the circumstances of the particular family that is seeking help. Some, such as Satir, compile a family life history during the first interview, often comparing each person's perspective on what are significant past family events.[6] Others, such as Gerald H. Zuk, would collect family history information with a primary focus on current family activities and functioning.[7] Others focus on the "here-and-now" and do not collect a formal family history at all.

THE FAMILY DIAGRAM OR "GENOGRAM"

Family counselors who decide to obtain a family history often use the technique of mapping three or more generations of a family on a family diagram that they draw on paper or on a chalkboard. This "genogram" provides an overall structural picture of that family by defining family membership and family boundaries.[8]

This diagram uses standardized symbols to represent individuals and their relationships. A hollow circle is drawn to represent a female and a square for a male. A marriage would be pictured by a horizontal line drawn between a circle and a square. That couple's children would be denoted by drawing a vertical line downward from the middle of that horizontal line (that is, their marriage). Two slanted lines cutting across the horizontal line indicates a divorce, and a remarriage is indicated by another horizontal line to the new partner's symbol.

Constructing a genogram in this way can be a low-threat method for obtaining information about the history of the family. The counselor starts out by asking identifying information such as names, ages, and careers. The important transitions of life—marriage, divorce, deaths, moves, and remarriages—are gathered along the way, and often important issues for counseling emerge in the process of writing down this family diagram, as family members reveal quarrels, family crises, and family secrets.

Whether the counselor chooses to use the genogram method or not, assessing a family's problems is the first step in counseling a family. The family counselor must pinpoint where the problems lie, and understanding the family's life history can assist in this assessment.

After drawing the genogram, the family counselor can ask further specific questions to obtain a more complete family history. This might be done in a session with the couple or individual sessions with the husband and wife, if they prefer. The following outline lists potential questions that could be covered; for a particular couple, you may want to select some of these questions or ask related questions that arise during the course of the interview.

Outline for Obtaining Family History Information[9]

I. Father's Family of Origin
  A. Could you describe your childhood relationship with your parents?
    1. How strong or weak was the bond between your parents and their children? How was the bond that you had with your parents different from that of your siblings?
    2. Did either of your parents prefer one child over another?
    3. Describe the disciplinary approaches of your mother and father. Was either of them overprotective? Was either overindulgent? Was either particularly restrictive? Was either harsh or demanding? Was either encouraging? Was either patient? kind? loving?
    4. What influence did your father and mother have on your moral and spiritual development as a child? as a teenager?
  B. Describe the marriage relationship between your parents.
    1. What were the strengths of their marriage?
    2. What were the weaknesses of their marriage? Was there any separation? divorce? infidelity? alcoholism or drug abuse? physical abuse? psychological abuse?
    3. Describe your father's spiritual life. And your mother's spiritual life. Did they attend church regularly? Did either of them lead the family in prayer? in devotions or Bible reading? Did either of them live the Christian life on a daily basis?
    4. What were your father's attitudes toward women? toward his wife?
    5. What were your mother's attitudes toward men? toward her husband?
  C. How did your parents influence your identity and sense of well-being?
    1. How did your parents treat the uniqueness and individual differences in each of their children?
    2. How did your parents help you develop a sense of individual responsibility and freedom?

---

    3. How did your parents help you develop your identity? Which parent did you identify with most? What qualities did you pick up from each parent?

    4. Do you seek parental approval of your decisions or activities since you have been married? Does either of your parents seem to intrude on your marriage? Does either dominate or interfere with your affairs since you have been married?

  D. How did your parents relate to their community?

    1. What were your father's and mother's relationships to the community? the church? the business or professional world?

    2. What was your family's reputation in the community?

    3. What was your family's socioeconomic status? standard of living? educational level? value for education of children? income level?

II. Mother's Family of Origin (use identical questions above in I.)

III. Marriage History and Chronology

  A. Previous marriages of husband and/or wife

    1. Was either of you previously married or previously a parent?

    2. What were the circumstances that ended that relationship?

    3. What children were born of that union? What are the custody arrangements? What are the child-support arrangements? What are the visitation schedules?

    4. What is the relationship of your former spouse with your present family?

  B. Tell me about your relationship before you were married.

    1. How did you meet? How long did you know each other before engagement? How long were you engaged before marriage?

    2. Did each of your parents approve of the marriage plans?

    3. Did either of you have any doubts about getting married?

    4. What were your prior dating and courting experiences?

    5. Did each of you regard yourself as adequately prepared for marriage?

    6. Did you have premarital sexual relations?

    7. What did each of you expect of the other before marriage? What were your expectations of marriage?

    8. What was your spiritual condition before marriage?

  C. Describe significant events in your marriage relationship in the past.

    1. What crises have you faced together?

    2. What events have revealed strengths in your relationship over time?

    3. What events have revealed weaknesses in your marital relationship?

    4. In what ways have you worked well together as parents?

    5. In what ways have you struggled in your parenting?

The Family as a System

When a family comes to a pastor or other family counselor, there is usually a presenting complaint. Some situation is described, but this may be just an irritation on the surface. Immediately you have the task of trying to determine what the underlying problem is.

To assess family problems that may lurk beneath the surface of the presenting problem, we need to understand the ways in which a family can malfunction. Whether it is normal or malfunctioning, the family is a system[10] consisting of people relating to one another over time. In fact, the family unit is the basic, primary human system in any society.

Picture the family as a decorative mobile hanging by a string from the ceiling. The string is connected to a long thin stick and there are other strings hanging down from each end of the stick. Each one has something else dangling down from it. A normal mobile is carefully balanced and has a certain equilibrium to it. If you come up to it and push one little element on the mobile, what happens? It affects the whole system. As that mobile settles down after having been touched, it regains equilibrium. Suppose you just cut one of the dangling objects off. What is that going to do to the system? It's going to change and be a little lopsided, right? This pictures the family as a system and how the system can be dysfunctional.

There are interlocking parts to the system. It's a set of interacting components that co-vary such that each element in the family is dependent on the functioning of the other elements in the family.

Family Rules

Just as the mobile functions by the laws of gravity, the family system is governed by rules. There are stated and unstated rules in the family that are understood by the family members.[11] These rules are not necessarily listed and posted on the refrigerator in the kitchen, but they are understood by the members as the family grows up, and these rules pattern the behavior in a family.

A few years ago, I had a bright and effective teaching assistant assigned to me at another university; her name was Donna Green and she happened to be a very dedicated Christian. She told me one day that she was invited to go home on a weekend with her roommate, another Christian girl in graduate school. So Donna stayed overnight at her friend's house and the family made her feel very welcome indeed. They showed her all the major sights in the town where they lived, a town she had never visited before. They were just so very nice to her that when she was leaving their house on Sunday evening to drive back up to the university, Donna exclaimed, "Thank you very much for such a nice weekend! I really enjoyed seeing the town." Then she spontaneously hugged the father of her friend as an expression of her gratitude. Well, the father immediately froze, becoming very rigid, and she immediately realized that she had violated a family rule. It was very awkward. Everyone stopped talking and stared at her.

This was a shock to Donna because, in her family, they often hugged and especially when she would leave to go off to the university. But in her roommate's family there was a rule, an unspoken rule. It was not posted anywhere, but this family did not hug. When she was driving back up to the university with her roommate, her roommate said, "You really startled my dad. He was really taken off guard. In our family we never hug like that, and he didn't know what to do with that."

There are all kinds of rules like this in families, and these rules determine certain kinds of patterns of family relationships. Often in assessing a family's underlying problems, the family counselor must look for these unwritten rules, bring them out in the open, and determine if a given rule is contributing to the problem at hand.

Family Boundaries

There are certain subsystems within the family that perform separate family functions. One obvious subsystem in the family is the marriage relationship. There might also be a father/son relationship operating as a subsystem, and there could be a father/daughter subsystem, a mother/son subsystem,

and a mother/daughter subsystem. The siblings may relate together in certain ways. The grandparents, aunts, uncles, and
cousins form the extended family subsystems. On occasion, a
family counselor will identify a major problem in a family subsystem and spend some counseling sessions with only members
of that subsystem.

Just as the whole family has its boundaries, these various
subsystems have their own boundaries.[12] For example, there
are certain boundary conditions of the marriage. The husband
and wife have parenting in common if they have children.
They have their own relationship that is going on at the same
time they are relating to the children. The boundaries delin-
eating each subsystem in the family need to remain clear and
enforced in a healthy, adapted, functioning family.

When the boundaries between family members become
blurred and members become overly involved in one another's
lives, the family is "enmeshed."[13] Someone once described the
difference between enmeshment and closeness this way: *Enmeshment* is like a bowl of pea soup where all the peas are
squashed and you can't tell one pea from another pea.[14] In a
normal, well-functioning family, togetherness is like a bowl of
individual peas, not soup. They're all in the same bowl—
they're in the same family—but you can see the individuality
of each member. They're not merged with one another. They
are close and they have a healthy togetherness, but it's not enmeshment. Enmeshment occurs when the individuality of the
members is lost. Sometimes counselors see a mother who can't
even talk about her preschool child without using the word
"we." "When *we* first entered kindergarten . . . when *we* went
to preschool." Such talk does not allow for an individual identity of each family member.

In extreme cases of enmeshment, a family member feels or is
told that any separation from the family would be a betrayal of
the family. When family membership is so overemphasized,
the individuals have genuine difficulty developing a separate
identity or a separate sense of themselves, and they are prone
to psychosomatic disorders.[15]

The opposite situation is where families have such rigid
boundaries separating them that they feel and behave isolated

from one another. A sense of closeness with the family is missing. These are called "disengaged families," and the children often grow up with difficulties in forming relationships with people outside the family as well.[16]

The family counselor will often assess a problem family and find that their boundaries have become foggy and unclear. Last year, I saw a family in which the older daughter was eleven and the younger daughter was eight. The father, Mr. Wade, was working full-time as a bureaucrat for a state agency. Because he was also working on his bachelor's degree in evening school, he was gone most of the time from his family. When he wasn't at work, he was off to class in the evening or at the library studying.

Mrs. Wade was a school teacher. She was trying to work full-time as a school teacher and also handle the girls at home. The girls displayed all kinds of behavior problems—failure to complete homework assignments, near constant bickering, refusal to complete household chores, pouting, throwing objects at one another, complaining, manipulating, and failing to get dressed in time for the school bus in the mornings (to mention only a few). The mother quit her job to try to manage the children better, and she requested family counseling.

It was difficult to arrange for Mr. Wade to come in because we had to work around his tight schedule. When the father did come with the rest of the family, he was very passive and noninvolved. The girls right away started complaining about each other. The older girl, Cathy, was quite overweight and the younger girl, Lisa, was thin and petite so she would criticize Cathy for being fat and "dumpy." "Cathy eats too much." "Cathy doesn't do her homework." "She doesn't make her bed." "She doesn't get up in time for the school bus." "I really think Mommy and Daddy should make her shape up and put her on a diet and make her pick up her room and behave."

No sooner would Lisa pause than Cathy would reply, "Lisa is just butting in all the time. Whenever Mom or Dad comes home and they are talking to me, she interrupts them and pretends like she's running the family." It became apparent after two family counseling sessions that the boundaries defining who is an adult or parent and who is a child were very foggy in this family.

The father passively let all this go on, while the mother would say, "I feel like I'm trying to manage and cope with a family with three children instead of two! My husband just acts like another child. He comes home, takes off his shoes, throws his shirt on the floor in the living room and watches TV. Then I'm trying to get after him to pick up after himself and do something with our daughters." The father assumed a kind of child's role. He didn't object to that, and seemed to want to be "mothered" by his wife.

Furthermore, the youngest daughter, Lisa, would yell at her mother, telling her what she ought to tell the dad to do. "You ought to tell *him* to cook dinner. You ought to tell *him* to sweep the floor. Why don't you tell him to come home sooner from the library? He ought to be home by 8:30. You shouldn't allow him to be out until 9:30." So then Mrs. Wade would say to Mr. Wade, "Yes, why don't you come in at 8:30." The next evening, Lisa would monitor Dad's compliance. She would watch the clock, and if he was not back by 8:30, she would say, "Dad, you were supposed to be here at 8:30 and here you're coming in at 8:45." The daughter was behaving almost like a parent monitoring a teenager who is supposed to be in by curfew. So the role boundaries between the subsystems in this family were fuzzy. The parent role and the child role were often reversed.

Family Roles

A lot of counseling work with families has been built on a role theory that developed in the field of sociology.[17] Each person in the family has some kind of role which has obligations and expectations attached to it. The mother might do certain things the father doesn't do and the father might do some things the mother doesn't do. For example, the father may mow the lawn, and he may fix the car, and over time this becomes expected of him. The kitchen might be the wife's domain. She may not want him to come in, open cupboards, and pull down items to cook a meal. Such roles vary from family to family.

But there may be some confusion in a family regarding roles. Perhaps the roles keep on shifting. It may not be clear who does what or there may be conflict over roles—for example, the father may usurp the mother's role. In the Wade family, the youngest daughter, Lisa, was usurping a parental role and this generated conflict.

Because the family is a system, each member's role has some complementary effect on other family members. Thus, if the father is carrying out an effective leadership role, that has an impact upon the child's role in that family.[18] When the father abdicates the leadership role, as in the Wade family, then a vacuum is created and the child's role may be unclear.

In a family where the roles are functioning in accordance with biblical standards, they have a positive complementary effect. For instance, a mother may show more modesty around her son than around her daughter, encouraging development of a positive complementary sex role. But on the other hand, roles can become stereotyped and inflexible in a problem family. If the son learns how to bathe himself and does it only part of the time, the family could let him get stuck in the role of the dependent little child who has to have Mommy bathe him all the time. He could become five, six, seven, eight, nine, ten, and somebody is still drawing water in the tub for him, washing his body, and thereby keeping him in a dependent, immature role.

So, family counseling often involves clarifying and modifying roles. It may focus on helping to develop positive complementary roles, trying to solve some of the conflicts in the roles, and clearing up confusion in the roles. One of the things my psychology students and I did with the Wade family was to videotape family sessions and let them see themselves interacting. They would get into a big argument over some issues, such as whether Cathy was making her bed or not and the younger daughter, Lisa, would complain, "Well, Cathy should fix it up before she leaves for school. She should get up at 6:30 A.M., and I also think Daddy should set a better example. If Daddy's not home by 8:30 P.M., he shouldn't be allowed to eat snacks that night." We played the videotapes back to the family and asked them different questions such as, "Who is the parent here? Who is taking the parent role?" And they developed a lot of insight into their problems by just watching their family interact on tape.

WHAT IS THE PROBLEM?

When a family comes in for counseling, often one person in the family is labeled as the problem. In the Wade family I have just described, the complaint was that the older daughter Cathy was moody, was not happy, and needed help. But as you have no doubt seen, the focus of the problem rested in the family relationships—how all the family members related to one another.

The mother would require Cathy to do certain things like cleaning up her room, but then again, it was an unwritten rule in this family that such "requirements" were ignored. It was understood that if you did not obey, Mother was not going to do anything about it. She didn't enforce her commands, and Cathy knew full well that she could get away with not complying.

Mother would go into Cathy's bedroom and say, "Cathy, get up. It's time to get up. If you don't get up right now, you're not going to be ready in time to eat breakfast before the school bus comes." And so Cathy would sleep in a little bit longer and mother would come in, get very upset, and say, "Cathy, I told you to get up and now you're going to miss the bus!" Cathy knew that if she missed the bus her mother would simply complain, "Now I'm going to have to drive you to school and this is going to make me late to work." (This was before Mrs. Wade quit her teaching job.) The only consequence for getting up late was that the mother would chauffeur Cathy individually. Mrs. Wade would even make sure she had something for overweight Cathy to eat in the car on the way, commenting, "You're not going to be able to get through school today unless you eat."

The younger daughter, Lisa, was actually calling most of the shots in this family. She was the more dominant of the daughters. She was playing the role of the "good child" who is victimized, and Cathy was playing the role of the "bad child." Lisa always cleaned up her side of the room, usually had her bed made, and always got up in time to catch the school bus. She regularly criticized Cathy for failure to do the same things, and she blamed Cathy for their bickering and her own pouting.

The "Identified Problem" versus the Real Problem

This counseling case illustrates that one individual in the family may be identified as the problem (in this case Cathy) when the problem actually resides in the entire family system. The Wade family experienced a confusion of role boundaries; there was a blurring of the appropriate parental roles and authority prescribed by Scripture (Ephesians 6:1–4; Proverbs 3:11–12; 22:15; 29:17).[19] The father should assume leadership over the family (Ephesians 5:21–33; Matthew 20:28; Colossians 3:18, 19; 1 Corinthians 11:3; Romans 13:1).[20] In the Wade family, the father was not exercising leadership and the mother had substantially lost control of the situation, creating a distorted family system. So, the leadership was either weak or vacillating. At one point, the father seemed to be in charge, but on the next day the mother seemed to be in charge or the leadership was just plain nonexistent. Frankly, there really was no true, consistent leadership in this family. This is frequently the case in problem families. With two parents working full-time, a lot of physical energy is expended outside the home and the parents often do not have the time it actually takes to lead their family. Family leadership takes a substantial investment of energy and time to carry out effectively. By asking careful questions, the family counselor can observe and assess the presence or absence of parental leadership and authority patterns in a family.

Family Scapegoating

In problem families, children may be assigned or choose to take roles inappropriate to their age, sex, or personality characteristics.[21] Sometimes the child takes on a parenting role. Sometimes the child is cast in a sexualized role or as a "family pet." Sometimes the child becomes the scapegoat. In this case, twelve-year-old Cathy was blamed for all the family's problems. Such roles become clear as the counselor asks each family member to describe significant family patterns at home.

Some families maintain equilibrium by defining one member

as the "sick" one, that is, the problem of the family.[22] Scapegoating is the process in which a family member is unconsciously chosen to manifest the symptoms of a dysfunctional family.[23] Scapegoating one family member often occurs when there is minimal interaction and minimal intimacy in the marriage relationship, and scapegoating therefore serves to keep a weak marriage from falling apart.

This was the case in the Wade family with their two girls. Mr. and Mrs. Wade were very remote from one another. The father was not participating in parenting, so the parental coalition was weak. The tensions between Mr. and Mrs. Wade were not resolved. But as a way to avoid expressing hostility to one another, this couple transferred their hostility to the older daughter who became the family scapegoat.

A child may even unconsciously pick up the expectation that he or she is supposed to be the "problem child" and will often act out that role and attempt to make the most of it. In the process, the scapegoated member develops a behavioral or emotional disorder. Cathy Wade, the twelve-year-old girl, was picking up that she was labeled the "problem child," and she complied by not making her bed, by not getting up in the morning, and by missing the school bus. As a result, she became the family scapegoat and the "identified patient" for counseling.

The parents projected their own emotional problems onto Cathy and then expressed overconcern for her problems. Cathy therefore received considerable attention, although much of that attention was negative. She wielded considerable power in the family and had much invested in maintaining her role as "the problem." If she had rejected her role as the problem, she would have lost attention and power and the family would have been disrupted. As the scapegoat, Cathy was absorbing stress so that her parents could function with less conflict and tension. Because her symptoms were the result of family scapegoating, family counseling was prescribed for her.

Individual Problems or Family Problems?

The family counselor needs to be alert to ways in which the individual personalities of family members may be contributing

Assessment Questions Regarding Individual Family Members[24]

I.   What is this person's level of emotional stability?
   A. Is there evidence of abnormal mood swings to depression and/or manic elation? Is there evidence of suicidal thoughts or plans?
   B. Is this person's behavior unusually impulsive or erratic?
   C. Is the person's expression of emotions inappropriate to the situation or topic of discussion?
   D. Are paranoid feelings or thoughts expressed?
   E. Is there evidence for abnormal sadistic or masochistic behavior?
   F. Does this person respond to the family in primarily emotional ways?

II. What is this person's level of maturity?
   A. Does this person evidence a level of maturity and responsibility appropriate for his or her development and age?
   B. Is this person excessively independent?
   C. Is this person abnormally dependent in relating to others?
   D. Does this person have an appropriate capacity to give and receive love, and is he or she living up to that capacity?
   E. Is this person extremely self-centered or selfish, beyond what is expected typically at his or her age?

III. How does this person characteristically relate to others?
   A. What psychological defense mechanisms are in evidence when this person encounters stress in relating to others? Rationalization? Denial? Projection of the person's own motives or faults on others? Conscious suppression of the conflict? Unconscious repression of the conflict?
   B. Is this person aware of his or her use of defense mechanisms?
   C. Is this person's level of anxiety interfering with relationships?
   D. Does this person have insight or a capacity of insight into the reasons for his or her style of interacting with family members?

IV. What is this person's level of intelligence?
   A. Does this person have any special intellectual talents or abilities?
   B. Does this person evidence any deficit in intellectual ability? Does this require formal testing by a clinical psychologist?
   C. Are any of the family problems caused in part because of this person's mental or educational limitations?

V.   What is this person's level of spiritual maturity and rate of growth?
   A. Does this person show evidence of a normal conscience in terms of sensitivity to guilt? Is there a level of moral insensitivity? Is there an extreme and inappropriate tendency to guilt feelings? Is there an appropriate repentant attitude regarding sin?
   B. Does this person regularly consider how God views his or her behavior?
   C. Is there a desire to please God above pleasing self or others?
   D. Does this person's current life give evidence of being totally committed to the Lordship of Jesus Christ as the result of having experienced salvation from sin? Is this person primarily motivated by love of God and love for others in daily life?
   E. Does this person value religious activities and rules in the absence of the predominant characteristics of love for God and others and concern for the truth of Scriptures?

to family problems or particularly to the distress of any individual. An attempt should be made to evaluate the personality traits and personality functioning of each family member. The questions that the family counselor should have in mind in making this evaluation are listed on the chart on page 47.

If an individual is experiencing emotional or mental distress of some type (anxiety, depression, anger, chronic frustration, etc.), should we consider the problem to be an individual problem or should we consider these as merely symptoms of a family problem? And, when a family comes to counseling with a dysfunction but also complains about distress in an individual, which came first—the individual problem or the family problem?

Extremists have answered these questions on both sides of the issue. On the one hand, there are the extreme family therapy advocates who claim that there is "no such thing as an individual mental disorder" but that all such complaints are really symptoms of family system problems.[25] They would say that the psychological distress experienced by an individual family member is merely reflecting a family problem. On the other hand, there are experts who have taken the opposite position, insisting that internal psychological conflicts become the cause for the distress in a family.[26] They recognize individual mental disorders and emotional disturbances and although they see family factors as perhaps contributing to the development of individual psychological problems, they view a psychological problem as something that requires treatment to be delivered to the individual experiencing the problem. If the individual's problem is cured, then the distress upon the family should be cleared up.

With regard to those two extreme positions, we can point out a few things from research. First, there is a relationship between marital conflict in couples and disorders in their children.[27] On the other hand, we also know from research that any change of any element in the family system will affect the other elements in that system.[28] A balanced way of viewing this is to acknowledge that family problems do exist, and individual problems do exist, and furthermore, there is considerable interrelationship between the two. This more realistic view acknowledges that both family system problems and individual psychological and spiritual problems can be occurring at the same time. An abnormal family relationship can contribute to the development of a mental or emotional disorder.[29] Furthermore, the individual with a psychological problem can create and contribute to family relationship problems.

For example, the depressed housewife might be failing to accomplish routine household chores of getting the laundry done, providing meals, purchasing groceries, and so on, thereby causing distress to the operation of the family system. At the same time, other features of family life may be contributing to the woman's depression, such as a dictatorial husband who attempts to control all the other family members through threats, verbal abuse, and physical violence. There is undoubtedly an interaction between individual psychological well-being and healthy family functioning. Some psychotic disorders (where the individual loses contact with reality) can be precipitated by physical causes. The family member who behaves in a psychotic way, in turn, creates tremendous stress upon the rest of the family members, and this may cause the family system to function poorly.

Americans, who tend to be very individualistic, need to be reminded that while Scripture calls for individual obedience, exhorting individuals to flee from sin (Job 11:14; 2 Timothy 2: 19, 22; Hebrews 12:4; 1 Corinthians 6:18; 1 Timothy 6:11), it also calls for corporate responsibility and requires that groups of individuals live according to their social obligations (Romans 13:3, 4; 1 Timothy 5:1–21). Therefore, there are both an individual morality and a family morality to be considered (see Appendix 3).

It is foolish, therefore, to take either of the two extreme positions, to say, "All problems are family problems. Therefore, the solution is always family counseling," or to say the opposite, "All problems are really problems of the individual. Therefore, individual counseling is preferred." It is best to admit that there is some truth in both of those positions, and sometimes even within a family the counselor might profitably recommend some individual counseling while continuing family counseling as well. At times, an individual has an adjustment problem and a counselor works with that person in a one-to-one relationship and that problem is cleared up. But then other family problems crop up because this dysfunctional family member was absorbed in some kind of adjustment the family made to achieve its own homeostasis or equilibrium. Solving that problem puts the family off-balance.

One very efficient way to find out whether a particular family member needs individual counseling or psychotherapy in addition to or instead of family counseling is to refer that individual for clinical psychological testing. Literally thousands of psychological tests have been developed in the twentieth century to assist the diagnosis of a myriad of problems, including personality disorders, developmental disorders, psychotic disorders, mood disorders, psychosexual dysfunctions, anxiety disorders, neuropsychological conditions, and other problems of mental functioning.[30] The family counselor (whether pastor, clinical social worker, psychiatrist, or other type of helping professional) should develop a relationship with one or more licensed clinical psychologists that he or she would feel comfortable referring individuals or families to for psychodiagnostic testing. Using the clinical psychologist as a consultant in this way can greatly enhance the counselor's assessment of families and help to target the counseling efforts appropriately.

Some family counselors may have familiarity with only a few personality tests, but it is unwise to administer the same test instrument to all counselees just because it is a test that one happens to be familiar with. Certainly we would not think much of a physician who prescribed aspirin to every patient because he or she was not familiar with a wider range of medications. Instead of doing a superficial or misdirected job of assessment with family members, it is best to refer to a qualified clinical psychologist who is trained in a wide spectrum of psychodiagnostic instruments and who can therefore choose from among the variety of tests to answer the specific assessment questions posed by a particular person's problems.

COMMUNICATION PROBLEMS

A major source of problems in a family has to do with communication patterns. Poor communication undermines family functioning. This can happen in a number of ways. First of all, communication involves one person expressing something while another person listens. So, normal family functioning involves members who are not only good at expressing thoughts and feelings, but also good at listening to one another.

Nick Stinnett illustrates this by telling a story about President Lincoln.[31] When Abraham Lincoln was president, he would often call for a friend back in Illinois whom he knew when he had a law practice. When facing some crisis or some major decision he had to make, Lincoln would call for this friend to visit him in the White House to consult with him. Back in those days, the President didn't have Air Force One to fly out to Illinois to give a friend a ride to the White House. So, the President would send out a buggy to go pick up his friend, who would ride for the days required and eventually arrive at the White House. Lincoln's friend would stay overnight in the White House, get up in the morning, and go downstairs to the President's office; and Lincoln would describe the dilemma he faced and the various options he had.

After Lincoln was assassinated, this friend wrote about his friendship with Lincoln and described his role as a presidential advisor. He wrote that his role was basically to be a good listener. He would just listen to Lincoln describe his options, and he would restate the options back to Lincoln or say, "Well, I hear you saying that you're very frustrated because on one hand the advantages of option A are X and Y, but on the other hand, the advantage of option B is Z, and you have to choose one or the other and you can't have both advantages." He would just listen and use what we now call "active listening." Eventually Lincoln would come to a decision and send his friend back home. This friend was a good listener.

Passive Listening and Ignoring

In the dysfunctional family, not only do we find deficits in family members being able to express their true feelings to one another, but we also find poor listeners. A lot of "passive listening" goes on at best, and ignoring one another at worst. Other family members can't tell the difference between passive listening and ignoring. If a teenager is not giving any feedback, the parents can't tell whether their words are registering or not.

Double Bind

Another kind of communication that occurs in some dysfunctional families is a discrepancy between the overt content of what is said and the covert message. We communicate not only by the words that we say—the verbal communication—but also by nonverbal meaning, by tone of voice, by gesturing, and the like. In strong, adaptive families there is congruence between the verbal message and the nonverbal message, but in many problem families double messages are often given. The overt content and covert message are different.

For example, with an edge of hostility in her voice, a mother says to her young child, "Come here, honey." And the child moves over toward the mother. Then as the child moves toward the mother, the mother backs away. She backs away and stiffens up rather than leaning down and reaching out toward the child. Responding to this nonverbal message, the child draws away from the mother. The mother has done three things. She said, "Come here." Those were her words, but her voice has indicated some hostility, and her motions are withdrawing from the child. But as the child responds by drawing away from the mother, the mother then says, "What's the matter, dear? Don't you love Mama?"

In this little interaction, you can see what Bateson has called the "double bind."[32] The child will lose either way. If the child comes toward the mother as the mother backs off and stiffens, there is real incongruity there, and the child feels uncomfortable. But if the child backs away, the mother gives this biting remark, "You don't love your mother." This is the kind of confused or irrational relationship we often see in mother/child relationships or father/child relationships in families with emotionally disturbed children. In the "double bind," the overt content and covert messages are discrepant.

Why did this happen? Sometimes families have conflicting needs or the family members have conflicting needs. Perhaps this mother is afraid of closeness, but on the other hand she knows she is supposed to be close to her child, so she's wanting the child to come and hug her. But another part of her is still rejecting that emotional closeness. So she gives a vague or conflicting communication to the child.

Weak Parental Coalitions

In a healthy, optimally functioning, competent family, members relate to one another in ways that are clearly distinguishable from the ways found in problem families. Good, clear communication patterns are evident in addition to the parents' cooperation.[33] In the Wade family, the parents were at odds with one another, and the mother actually considered the father as just another child. In the competent family, the parents function together as a coalition in their parenting responsibilities.

In contrast, the dysfunctional family typically has poor communication patterns and an inconsistent or weak parental coalition. The parents do not work very well together. Sometimes parents use different discipline approaches. The child quickly learns, "If you don't like the answer you got from Mom, go to Dad and maybe you'll get a different answer." It's all too easy for a child to play one parent against the other when the parents are not working as a team. A family counselor can assess family communication patterns and parental coalition patterns by asking various family members how the parents give instructions to children and what happens if a child does not respond.

There are a variety of ways in which couples can experience difficulty in parenting their children together in an effective and cooperative way. The counselor may find it helpful to use the following checklist to evaluate the parenting practices of a couple. The items on this checklist are problems which are frequently observed in the course of counseling families. The more items checked, the greater the complexity and seriousness of the family's problem. Some of these problems can be ruled out by simply watching the parents interact with their children; others can be ruled out or detected only by asking specific questions of the couple and/or the children regarding the parent-child relationships.

Counselor's Checklist on Potential Problems in Parenting[34]

I. Problems in Loving Children Appropriately
_____ Father fails to verbally express love to children regularly
_____ Mother fails to verbally express love to children regularly
_____ Father has poor eye-to-face contact with children
_____ Mother has poor eye-to-face contact with children
_____ Father fails to provide physical hugs, pats, and affectionate touch
_____ Mother fails to provide physical hugs, pats, and affectionate touch
_____ Father behaves self-centeredly and selfishly toward family
_____ Mother behaves self-centeredly and selfishly toward family

II. Problems in Exercising Parental Authority
_____ Father fails to assume a proper parental role
_____ Mother fails to assume a proper parental role
_____ Child assumes a parental role (Name child: _____)
_____ Father undermines mother's parental authority
_____ Mother undermines father's parental authority
_____ Parents are divided on disciplinary methods and consequences
_____ Father's rules are rigid and inappropriate for child's developmental level
_____ Mother's rules are rigid and inappropriate for child's developmental level
_____ Father is inappropriately permissive
_____ Mother is inappropriately permissive

III. Problems in Establishing Clear Limits for Children
_____ Father fails to communicate reasonable limits for child behavior
_____ Mother fails to communicate reasonable limits for child behavior
_____ Parents disagree on standards for child behavior
_____ Father is inconsistent in adhering to his own standards for children
_____ Mother is inconsistent in adhering to her own standards for children

---

_____ Children are not taught acceptable behavior for social situations

_____ Father administers discipline in harsh, unloving manner

_____ Mother administers discipline in harsh, unloving manner

_____ Children appear afraid of father

_____ Children appear afraid of mother

_____ Children often are angry at father

_____ Children often are angry at mother

_____ Child's behavior is uncontrolled in terms of what is usually expected at a given developmental age

IV. Problems in Treating Children as Individuals

_____ Father prefers one child over another

_____ Mother prefers one child over another

_____ Father critically compares one child to another

_____ Mother critically compares one child to another

_____ Father does not express acceptance of differences in children in intelligence, personality traits, physical appearance, talents, abilities, interests, etc.

_____ Mother does not express acceptance of child differences (see above)

_____ Father expects child achievement beyond child's actual capacity

_____ Mother expects child achievement beyond child's actual capacity

_____ Father fails to encourage children

_____ Mother fails to encourage children

_____ Father sees a child primarily as an extension of himself

_____ Mother sees a child primarily as an extension of herself

_____ One child is rejected by father _____ or by mother _____

_____ One child is overindulged by father _____ or by mother _____

Competent families are also flexible as they progress through the developmental life cycle. As certain kinds of relationships in the family become outmoded because children are getting older, parents and children adapt to different roles. The parent of a preschooler actually chooses the clothes for the child to wear, puts the clothes on the child, ties the child's shoes, and zips up the coat. As that child gets a little bit older, then he or she is given more and more responsibility in dressing.

My own five-year-old is in a transition phase in tying his own shoes. He can do it now, but he still prefers to have Mommy or Daddy do it for him. Often he will revert to the role of being a little, helpless preschooler like his little brother who can't tie his shoes yet. When Grandpa and Grandma came to visit, he took his little shoes over to Grandpa and had him put his socks and shoes on.

Problem families display various degrees of inflexibility. Role relationships are hard for them to revise as they move through the development phases. There are hidden conflicts, and often brute intimidation is used instead of negotiation. The parents try to intimidate their children, and the children thereby learn to intimidate one another.

Marital problems may also interfere with effective parenting cooperation. The following checklist can help guide such an assessment.

Counselor's Checklist on Potential Marital Problems in a Family[35]

I. Problems in Giving or Receiving Affection
　____ Husband fails to express affection
　____ Wife fails to express affection
　____ Husband regards wife's demands for affection as excessive
　____ Wife regards husband's demands for affection as excessive
　____ Affection is given as a reward for spouse's "good" behavior
　____ Affection is withheld from spouse as a punishment
　____ Husband denies he needs or wants affection from wife
　____ Wife denies she needs or wants affection from husband

II. Problems in Family Role Functioning
　____ Husband is insecure in masculine identification
　____ Wife is insecure in feminine identification
　____ Husband fails to take a leadership role
　____ Husband fails to be loving in leadership; acts as a dictator
　____ Wife asserts the dominant leadership role
　____ Wife fails to be appropriately submissive to husband
　____ Wife is inappropriately passive toward husband
　____ Husband demands his wife be submissive in inappropriate ways
　____ Husband undermines wife's role with children
　____ Wife undermines husband's role with children
　____ Husband is emotionally distant or underinvolved with children
　____ Wife is emotionally distant or underinvolved with children
　____ Husband and wife disagree on each other's roles in the home
　____ Husband criticizes wife's role in family in front of children
　____ Wife criticizes husband's role in family in front of children
　____ Wife emasculates the husband, undermining his masculinity
　____ Husband devalues wife's feminine contributions to the home

---

III. Problems in Resolving Conflicts
___ Solutions are reached impulsively, without adequate discussion
___ Husband fails to consider his decisions in view of the best interests of other family members
___ Wife fails to consider her decisions for family's best interests
___ Husband manipulates wife into a position of blame
___ Wife manipulates husband into a position of blame
___ A lack of mutual responsibility of husband and wife for the solution of family problems
___ Denial of conflict by husband ___ or by wife ___
___ Avoidance of conflict by husband ___ or by wife ___
___ Conflicts left unresolved over time

IV. Problems in Spiritual Life
___ Husband is unbeliever
___ Wife is unbeliever
___ Husband fails to provide spiritual leadership in the home
___ Wife fails to cooperate with husband's spiritual leadership
___ Religious life appears to be a mere formality
___ Disagreements between husband and wife regarding faith issues
___ Husband has inconsistency between beliefs and his behavior (Specify)
___ Wife has inconsistency between beliefs and her behavior (Specify)

Identifying Communication Problems

Communication problems are certainly common in troubled families, and the counselor will want to identify the specific difficulties experienced by the family coming in for counseling. While the checklist on the next page is by no means exhaustive, it could be useful in guiding the counselor's diagnosis.

FAULTY FAMILY BALANCE

A process continually takes place to maintain the emotional balance in the home through shifting patterns of interaction between family members. In any family a variety of emotional needs are being balanced out. How is this accomplished? Family theorists have identified several processes that families use to maintain their balance, like the little mobile that achieves a

Counselor's Checklist of Family Communication Problems[36]

____ Passive listening or ignoring family members occurs* _____

____ Double-bind messages are sent (verbal and nonverbal messages conflict) _____

____ Messages have hidden meanings _____

____ Messages have obscure meaning _____

____ Messages have ambiguous meanings _____

____ One or more family members are silenced _____

____ Silence is used against a family member _____

____ A family member withdraws from communicating _____

____ A family member attempts to disqualify self _____

____ A family member attempts to disqualify another from talking _____

____ A family member habitually fails to disclose thoughts or feelings _____

____ A family member appears unable to express feelings _____

____ A family member uses excessive anger or hostility _____

____ A family member uses condescending language regarding another family member _____

____ A family member withholds affectionate statements _____

____ A family member fails to express appreciation _____

____ Family members fail to use "active listening" (paraphrasing the other person's thoughts and feelings back to him or her) _____

____ A family member makes intimidating statements _____

____ A family member habitually raises voice with emotion _____

____ A family member tends to use critical remarks _____

____ Describe the family's typical communication problems here:

_____

*If a pattern of problem communication is checked, indicate which family members are involved in the space after the item description new equilibrium after something has disturbed it. Five faulty ways a family can maintain balance are emotional divorce, overadequate-inadequate balance, collusive alignment, splitting off, and surface peace.

Emotional Divorce

Bowen identified a process he called "emotional divorce."[37] In some families, the members keep one another at a "safe" emotional distance in order to avoid conflict. To avoid disagreement, they don't express strong emotions to one another. The husband and wife may become emotionally detached from one another. One parent, perhaps the mother, might develop a close relationship with a child and become very distant from the father. The father may withdraw from that child. By trying to avoid any outward conflict, family members achieve a kind of balance by becoming "emotionally divorced" from one another.

Overadequate-Inadequate Balance

Bowen identified another family pattern to maintain emotional balance between parents which he called "overadequate-inadequate pattern."[38] In such a situation, the mother may take over leadership while the father withdraws and becomes passive. She becomes "overadequate," compensating for his being "inadequate," and there is an interlocking relationship between these two roles. (An example would be the dominant wife and the alcoholic husband.) In other cases, the father leads while the mother withdraws. Sometimes this pattern occurs between a parent and a child. The parent might always dress a daughter even when she has learned to dress herself. This keeps the child helpless and inadequate, while the parent is taking an overadequate role.

Alignment and Splitting Off

As we have seen, balance is one of the operating principles of a system, and the family operates as a system in the sense that what one family member is doing has an impact on all the others. Dysfunctional families sometimes maintain a kind of faulty balance by forming an alignment between two members or by splitting off another family member.[39]

Here's an example. The Jennings family has a teenage girl, Linda, a teenage boy, Tom, a mother and father. Mr. Jennings and Tom begin talking at the dinner table and, sensing that his dad is in a good mood, Tom works up the nerve to say that he'd really like to have permission to drive the family car: "After all, I'm taking driver's training, and I already have a driver's permit. I could go pay for my driver's license after finishing driver's training."

His father pauses, and then replies by thinking out loud, "Well, maybe we could let you get your license if we could work out some arrangement. Would you be willing to pay for the gas if we let you borrow the car to go some place?"

Tom's eyes brighten up with enthusiasm. "Yeah, if I could go down and get my license next month, I'd have enough money. I would like to drive to the first school football game . . ."

Observing the father and son drawing close together, the mother interjects right in the middle of Tom's sentence with a comment meant to split off the son from the father by generating a conflict: "But if you let Tom have the car, you'll also have to let Linda drive the car. That would only be fair, and you know that Linda can't be trusted because of her recent shenanigans. You know that we've been telling her to get in by 11:00 P.M. and she hasn't been coming in on time. There is no way we can trust her, so there is no way that Tom can drive the car, because if we let him we have to let Linda have it too, and Linda is not responsible." This remark diverts the father's attention from Tom to Linda.

Linda debates, "No, I can too be trusted. You ought to let me drive the car, too. If you'd just let me do more grown-up things, I would act more grown-up."

Now the father gets heavily involved in a discussion with Linda and with the mother, and meanwhile, Tom is split off from the whole conversation. Tom started out negotiating with his father to get his license and be allowed to drive the family car. But the mother has diverted them, and the father, not wanting to disagree with his wife, has abandoned the discussion with the son.

These patterns of alignment and splitting off are dynamic things. Different alignments are set up from hour to hour, day

to day, week to week, or month to month, and in the dysfunctional family this means that another family member is being
split off and left out. The Jennings family achieved some balance by this artificial means, but it also produced confused
and chaotic relationships.

Surface Peace

In some cases, a family will develop a set of surface alignments that serve to blur or cover over underlying problems or
disagreements. Such a family might appear to be free of major
conflicts, but upon closer inspection the family counselor observes that family interactions are avoiding the real issues in
order to maintain the surface appearance of getting along.
Family members thus avoid the discomfort of more intimate relationships. "Surface peace" describes this way of maintaining
family balance.[40]

Here is a situation. In a family session, a mother was talking
about her teenage daughter, "I think Julie is old enough to
start dating on the condition that we approve of her boyfriend
as someone who is good for her to associate with."

With mild exasperation, Julie complained, "Well, Mother,
I've been wanting to date Bill but you've always said, 'No, you
can't date Bill,' just because you don't happen to like Bill.
Well, *I* think he's a terrific guy. I don't see why I can't date
Bill. I don't see anything wrong with him."

The mother quickly replied, "Well, actually it was your father who objected to Bill. Your father said he didn't want you
dating Bill."

After a brief pause to reflect, the father insisted, "Well, it's
not so much really that I object to Bill. There's nothing about
Bill per se. In fact, what I remember when you brought up Bill,
was that I just asked you to ask your mother what she thought
about Bill, and actually I probably said that your mother is a
good judge of men. After all, she married me, so why don't you
get your mother's opinion. That's what I remember. I don't remember saying anything against Bill."

With a loud sigh, Julie exclaimed, "But when I asked Mom,
she said to ask you, Dad!"

Mother quickly interjected, "Well, I think your father and I pretty much agree on the type of boy you should be associated with. Really, I think you ought to be thinking about dating Andy. Andy is a very nice young man and he's asked you out. Why don't you date Andy?"

With her eyes rolling upward, Julie shook her head, "Oh, I would never date him. He's a drip. He's no fun at all."

Then, attempting to smooth over the conversation, the mother said, "Well, I think that if we talk about it you would agree with Dad and me, at least most of the time anyway. Maybe you don't agree this time, but most of the time you would agree with us."

What is going on here is a family conversation that is avoiding the real issue—namely, what are the qualities of a boyfriend that the parents would find acceptable? In this conversation, the parents are not defining for Julie the characteristics of acceptable boys. They are talking all around the issue. The father is trying not to disagree with anybody. He is trying not to disagree with Julie. He is trying not to disagree with his wife. He is trying to avoid conflict and maintain a "surface peace," but in doing this, he is avoiding the real issue. If the parents began a frank discussion of what are desirable characteristics of a boyfriend, conflict would probably result because Julie has a different idea of what she wants in a boyfriend than the mother or maybe the father has. So, they are achieving a kind of balance in the family relationship by avoiding the issue here.

ROOTS OF FAMILY PROBLEMS

When biblical principles of family relationships are not followed, family problems will inevitably result. This is true to a degree whether the individual family members are Christians or nonbelievers. Even in a family in which all members are non-Christians, some degree of healthy, adaptive family functioning is possible if the family members are knowingly or unknowingly following the biblical principles of family relationship including, for example, supporting the leadership role of the father and husband, acting in loving ways to one another, behaving patiently, and forgiving one another.

Just as there are physical laws in the physical world, there are psychological and spiritual laws of family relationships. A person can function well physically by following the physical laws of the universe. For example, a person can avoid jumping off tall buildings and thereby survive physically even though that person may not be able to explain the physics of the law of gravity and even though the person may not know the Creator God who is the author of the law of gravity. In the same way, God has created certain laws and principles of relationship. When followed, these lead to positive outcomes. When the Christian or non-Christian person violates the laws of relationship carefully laid down in Scripture, relationship problems naturally result.

There are two roots of family problems—(1) deliberate or undeliberate sin by a family member, and (2) the effects of sin and the effects of living in a fallen world. On the one hand, it is obvious that an individual family member can sin by breaking one of God's commands in Scripture. The sin is generally some form of failing to love another family member in a specific situation. On the other hand, family problems are also caused by the indirect results of sin or the indirect results of living in a fallen world.

For example, a father, such as Mr. Wade, may fail to exert proper leadership and discipline in his relationship with his children because of a weak self-concept resulting from having been severely criticized and inconsistently disciplined or physically abused as a child. As a result of having had a poor fathering model himself, he has not naturally learned how to behave as a Christian father, and he has very little confidence in his own judgments with regard to disciplinary matters. This is a result of his own parents having sinned against him.

In other cases, family problems can result from the general presence of evil in the world. The untimely death of a young father of three children might be the result of a natural disaster or a genetic illness. The death of the young father may place a stress on the family system by creating a single-parent family without adequate financial resources. The mother may experience a role overload trying to handle the child-rearing responsibilities, household responsibilities, and responsibilities for income production all by herself. While it is possible to have a healthy, adaptive single-parent family in such a case, achieving such an adjustment is commonly a major problem, particularly in the first two years after the loss of the spouse.[41] Unless there is massive outside assistance from extended family, the community, and the church, the single-parent family is at high risk for a variety of family problems due to the abnormal handicap of being deprived of the other parent.[42]

SUMMARY

In conclusion, many problems experienced by families are a result of failing to live according to biblical principles of human relationships. Not every distressed family exhibits all of the possible family problems we've reviewed. However, the various family problems can feed into one another so that a family might be manifesting several problems at the same time.

It should also be said that it is difficult to isolate these family problems. By the same token, it is difficult to separate out the components of the strong, healthy, adaptable family. All the components are intermixed.

The family counselor distinguishes between the "identified problem" that the family initially presents and the underlying problem. In observing how a family operates like an interlocking system, the family counselor asks questions that clarify (1) the family rules, (2) the family boundaries (clear or enmeshed or disengaged), and (3) the family roles (including leadership roles, parenting roles, scapegoating roles). Among the communication problems which may exist are (1) passive listening, (2) ignoring one another, (3) double messages, and (4) weak parental coalitions. Every family system maintains either a healthy balance or a faulty balance, and the counselor should be aware of five common types of faulty family balance: (1) emotional divorce, (2) overadequate-inadequate pattern, (3) alignment, (4) splitting off, and (5) surface peace. Because the roots of all family problems are (1) sin or (2) the effects of living in a fallen world, the Christian family counselor should assess the spiritual condition of individual family members and of the family as a whole.

A final checklist summarizes these family interaction problems. This checklist can be used in conjunction with the others presented in this assessment chapter.

Counselor's Checklist on Family Interaction Problems

____ Family Rule Problems
    ☐ Specify:

____ Boundary Problems
    ____ Enmeshment
    ____ Disengagement
Note location of boundary problems: husband/wife, father/son, father/daughter, mother/son, mother/daughter, or extended family members.

____ Family Role Problems
    ☐ Specify:

____ Family Scapegoating
    ☐ Specify who is scapegoat:

____ Communication Problems (see separate checklist)
____ Parenting Problems (see separate checklist)
____ Marital Problems (see separate checklist)
____ Individual Psychological/Spiritual Problems (see separate checklist)
____ Emotional Divorce
____ Overadequate-Inadequate Balance
____ Alignment
____ Splitting Off
____ Surface Peace

CHAPTER THREE

BIBLICAL PERSPECTIVES
FOR GOAL SETTING

WHEN MRS. WADE FIRST CALLED ME on the phone to make an appointment, she complained about her older daughter, Cathy, who was overeating, getting emotionally upset frequently, and failing to make her bed. She was also telling her mother, "I hate you, I hate you, and I know that you hate me!" At first, the mother's goal was to obtain help for her daughter who seemed to her to be the problem in the family.

As we discussed the Wade family in chapter 2, we saw how important it is for the family counselor to accurately assess a family so that he or she may detect the underlying problems in the family system. What the family has identified as the main problem may not be what the counselor considers

66

the main need for counseling. In the Wade family, there was a confusion of role boundaries between parents and children. Although the parents had not identified the younger daughter, Lisa, as a problem, it was discovered that she was inappropriately taking on a parent role within the family dynamics.

Early in the process of family counseling, the counselor and the family need to come to some agreement as to the major goals of counseling. This often involves a process of negotiation. In the case of the Wade family, unless the counselor and family agree that some part of the problem resides in the family as a whole, the parents might be quite puzzled, if not surprised, when the counselor asks them to bring Lisa, in addition to Cathy, for the counseling appointment.

It is often quite useful for the family counselor to meet together with the entire family for the first counseling session. If the parents have some sensitive information they wish to share about a younger child without that child or the siblings being present, it is always possible to spend a portion of the first meeting with the parents alone. In the first session, the family counselor hopes to accomplish at least three things.

1. The counselor wants to observe the family as it describes its own problems. How do the family members relate to one another as they describe a problem situation? What seem to be the underlying problems in family dynamics which give rise to the complaints about individual family members?

2. After gaining some initial impressions of the dynamics of the family system, the counselor hopes to be able to sensitize the individuals to the ways in which they are functioning in a problematic manner. Then he or she hopes to use this information to begin negotiating counseling goals.

3. The counselor needs to formulate a strategy before the end of the first session which would help determine whether the whole or a part of the family should be scheduled for the next counseling session.

Of course, the overarching goal for all families is to help them improve their functioning as interdependent groups. In this sense, counselors have the hope that everyone in the given family will eventually benefit from the counseling process. As a practical matter, after counselors have been able to observe how families naturally present their set of problems to them, they may want to ask the individuals to describe what changes they desire to see in their family life. This process not only helps families focus on why they are coming in for counseling, but it also helps in the formulation of counseling goals. Immediately, counselors can observe if there is any conflict of goals among family members. Individual family members must cooperate with one another to arrive at their mutually held goals for counseling. Also, a collaboration process occurs between the family and the counselor in setting these goals. It becomes immediately apparent that the values held by individual family members and by the counselor will influence the selection of counseling goals. In turn, any individual's particular set of values will reflect that person's world view or faith system.

WHAT AMERICANS BELIEVE

For family counselors working in the United States, it is essential to recognize that a significant majority of the population holds to a theistic world view which influences, in varying degrees, the values held by individuals regarding family life.

In his book, *Democracy in America,* published in 1840, Alexis de Tocqueville observed, "It was religion that gave birth to the English colonies in America. One must never forget that. In the United States religion is mingled with all the national customs and all those feelings which the word Fatherland evokes. For that reason, it has peculiar power." More recently, George Gallup's polls have documented a high and stable level of religious belief in the American public. At Easter 1983, the Gallup Poll released data from its national survey that indicated that 87 percent of the American people believe that Jesus Christ has influenced their lives. Seventy-eight percent reported that they believed that Jesus was divine, and 60 percent stated that belief in Jesus Christ is "absolutely necessary" to the true knowledge of God. Seventy-two percent reported their belief that the Bible is the Word of God.

In a 1976 Gallup Poll, 38 percent of the American people said that the Bible should be taken literally as the Word of God, and 42 percent reported that they had attended church in the past seven days. These identical results were obtained four years later in 1980. Garry Willis appropriately observed, "Gallup's religious polling over the years is astonishing not for fluctuation, but for stability."[1]

According to the large study of the American population published in *The Connecticut Mutual Life Report on American Values in the '80s: The Impact of Belief*, "the level of religious commitment of Americans provides *the* key to understanding their values and behavior."[2] This national study conducted by Connecticut Mutual Life found the following:

- 44 percent of all Americans say they attend church frequently while 74 percent consider themselves religious.
- 49 percent of Americans report that there was a specific time in adult life when they made a personal commitment to Christ that changed their lives.
- 28 percent report frequently reading the Bible, while another 47 percent read the Bible occasionally.
- 73 percent of the American people frequently feel that God loves them and another 21 percent have this feeling occasionally.
- 57 percent frequently engage in prayer and another 32 percent occasionally engage in prayer.
- 90 percent of the American public report a Christian religious affiliation (62 percent Protestant and 28 percent Catholic); 2 percent report as Jewish, 4 percent list other religious affiliations, and 4 percent report no religious affiliation.
- 94 percent of Americans reported in 1948 that they believed in God (according to research then) and this percentage has remained constant up to the 1980s.[3]

The American population, by and large, also holds very strong beliefs regarding the value of family life. The research indicates that Americans consider interpersonal relationships, and family relationships in particular, as tremendously important to their lives:

- 79 percent rated sharing personal feelings with a spouse or intimate companion as very important to them, while an additional 16 percent rated this as somewhat important.
- 74 percent rated "doing things as a family group" as very important; another 22 percent rated this as somewhat important.
- 69 percent rated "playing with the children" as very important; another 24 percent rated this as somewhat important.
- 67 percent rated "talking to older members of your family" as very important; an additional 26 percent rated this as somewhat important.[4]

The researchers who summarized the national survey for the Connecticut Mutual Life Report concluded, "More than anything, Americans in the 1980s seem to want commitment in their relationships."[5] According to the report, 52 percent of the American public believe that divorce should be more difficult to obtain than it is now, and only 21 percent believe it should be easier to obtain. Forty-four percent reported that they would try to reconcile marital problems at all costs if unhappily married, whereas the other 56 percent were prepared to try to work it out, but would allow for a divorce if they did not succeed.

When the American people were asked to indicate their preference from among four lifestyles,

Sixty-three percent preferred an equal *marriage of shared responsibility* in which the husband and wife cooperate on working, homemaking and child-raising.

Twenty-nine percent preferred a *traditional marriage* in which the husband is responsible for providing for the family, and the wife for taking care of the home and the children.

Five percent preferred remaining *single*.

Three percent preferred *living with someone* without marriage.[6]

Eighty percent of the women and 75 percent of the men reported they would make at least one career sacrifice to raise their children.

Research indicates that American people with the highest levels of religious commitment place greater importance on the full range of family and friendship activities:

- 93 percent of the highly religious said it is very important to do things as a family group compared to 58 percent of the least religious.
- 71 percent of the most religious said they frequently visit family and relatives compared to 40 percent of the least religious.
- 80 percent of the most religious indicated they want to spend time talking with the older members of their families compared to 52 percent of the least religious.
- 64 percent of the most religious said they derive satisfaction from their immediate families compared to 39 percent of the least religious.
- 41 percent of the most religious favored a traditional marriage compared to 16 percent of the least religious.
- 60 percent of the most religious said they feel that an unhappy marriage should be reconciled at all costs compared to 33 percent of the least religious.[7]

In a study published by the Princeton Religion Research Center and the Gallup organization,[8] the following findings were reported:

- 78 percent of the churched and 38 percent of the unchurched say that they have made a commitment to Jesus Christ.
- 89 percent of the churched and 64 percent of the unchurched believe that Jesus Christ is God/the Son of God.
- 93 percent of the churched and 68 percent of the unchurched believe in the resurrection of Jesus Christ.
- 98 percent of the churched and 76 percent of the unchurched report that they pray to God. Seventy-four percent of the churched and 45 percent of the unchurched pray once a day or more, and an additional 19 percent of the churched and 34 percent of the unchurched pray less than once a day.

- 95 percent of the churched and 74 percent of the unchurched want their own children to receive religious instruction.
- 41 percent of the adults in this study were classified as unchurched while 59 percent were classified as churched (that is, having attended church other than on a holiday, and are members of a church).

These research findings clearly demonstrate that the American public is highly religious and predominantly Christian in its world view. The stronger the religious commitment in America, the stronger the family values, both in terms of belief and behavioral practice. This means that a large proportion of the American public derives its value system from the Christian Scriptures and that the ethical and spiritual principles governing human relationships as taught in the Bible provide a framework for family-life values for the majority of Americans. Both church attenders and nonchurch attenders are highly influenced by the Bible's teachings regarding marriage and family life. Family counselors need to recognize this fact and will expect family members to be consciously or unconsciously influenced by biblical values. This knowledge must of necessity influence the counselor's formulation of counseling goals.

It is, therefore, of strategic importance for the Christian family counselor to have an excellent grasp of biblical principles regarding family relationships because these principles directly influence the goals of the highly religious, committed families they serve. They also have a considerable impact upon the values of even unchurched Americans, the majority of whom hold to Christian beliefs.

BIBLICAL VALUE PERSPECTIVES

The Christian counselor has faith in the constant availability and sovereign goodness of God, upon which the family can rely for its effective functioning. This biblical perspective of family life includes such foundational concepts as: no one can serve two masters (one of which is God), a person should not be anxious for the necessities of life, and people should be committed to the things of the Spirit and God's kingdom above all else (Matthew 6:24–33).

The Christian counselor views spiritual roots as the source out of which other needs in life are met (Luke 6:43, 45). For this reason, he or she would endorse the practice of the vast majority of people in America who turn to God in prayer with their needs (Luke 11:9–13; Matthew 8:8–10; James 1:5–8). Therefore, faith in God and in his active involvement in our family life is a basic presupposition of the Christian counselor and of a significant majority of Americans.

God's Purpose for the Family

This Christian world view holds that we can know of God's work, including his creation of the family, both through general revelation (which would embrace human investigation by scientific studies) and, more fully, through special revelation (the Scriptures). Therefore, the Christian counselor approaches the family on the basis of his or her knowledge obtained from the social sciences under the authority of Scripture.[9]

In biblical revelation, God has revealed himself in three persons—Father, Son, and Holy Spirit. He has existed before the creation of humanity and possesses the personality and character qualities of love, nurture, creative vitality, and final authority, and is judge of our lives as individuals and as family members. God's character of love and holiness becomes our ultimate pattern for human relationships. Love and perfect communication existed among the three persons of the Trinity before the creation of human beings. When God established the family by first creating Adam, and then Eve, as individuals, and by joining them in marriage, he instituted the family relationship as a lifelong covenant of commitment. This commitment was to be to one another as well as to God whom man and woman would serve together (Genesis 2:21–24).

This means that the Christian counselor understands the definition of family relationships as those that are created by heterosexual marriage, by blood, by lineage, or by adoption. The biblical world view does not recognize any other definition of the family, such as the sharing of a dwelling by unrelated persons, or of homosexuals living together as though they were married. In the biblical world view, the family is not seen as an entity resulting from a mere social contract of convenience invented by human beings. Instead, the family is viewed as the first human institution ordained by God, designed to reflect God's image on the earth and created as the environment in which humankind is to fulfill God's commandment to further propagate the human race (Genesis 1:26–28; 2:21–25; Psalm 127:1; Proverbs 18:22; 2 Corinthians 6:14; Hebrews 13:4).

Love and Unity in the Family

A very important goal follows from this world view with regard to efforts in family counseling: Individual family members should not pursue individualistic objectives at the expense of the total family. Instead, the counselor should help the family live together on a daily basis with a unity of purpose, with a sense of unity between the husband and wife which transcends and, in fact, coordinates the exercise of individual differences and individual gifts (Genesis 2:18–25; Song of Solomon 8:7; Proverbs 31:20; Romans 15:1, 2; Ephesians 5:31; Matthew 19:5; Mark 10:7, 8).[10]

Many family problems that come to a counselor are a reflection of selfish attitudes on the part of specific members in a family. These selfish attitudes can be identified as the underlying problems contributing to disruptions in family unity, to difficulties parents experience in forming a workable coalition in their parenting, and to the neglect of other family members' needs. By contrast, the Christian world view affirms that love exercised through the power of the Holy Spirit should be the overriding principle for all family relationships. And this biblical form of love should be expressed in word and deed, regardless of the behavior, attitudes, or circumstances of other family members. This kind of love is manifested when a person puts the other family members' needs before his or her own (John 15:12; 13:35; 1 Corinthians 13; Colossians 3:14; Philippians 2:1–4). Matthew 10:20 and John 14:12–17 teach that it is God's Spirit who supplies wisdom and love, qualities necessary for effective family relationships (Galatians 5:13–26).

A relationship with God enables a person to manifest the

same qualities that Jesus exhibited in his relationships with people, when he lived on the earth (John 15). God's love for the individual empowers a person to creatively love others in the family (see John 17:20–24, 26). The Bible teaches that when God redeems people and indwells their lives, certain characteristics result from God's working: love, peace, patience, kindness, joy, goodness, gentleness, faithfulness, and self-control. Likewise, certain traits are lacking: jealousy and envy, selfishness and rudeness, irritability and the holding of grudges. The presence of these good characteristics and the absence of the negatives promote quality relationships in families. The Christian family counselor should make it his or her goal to encourage the spiritual development of persons who would yield these positive fruits in practical daily life.

In the value system endorsed by the Bible, a person's first commitment should be to God; commitments to people are secondary to this prior claim. Instead of pursuing "self-fulfillment," Christians are to commit themselves to God and to others. They experience personal fulfillment as a by-product of those prior commitments. Jesus taught, "'"Love the Lord your God with all your heart and with all your soul and with all your mind." This is the first and greatest commandment. And the second is like it: "Love your neighbor as yourself." All the Law and the prophets hang on these two commandments'" (Matt. 22:37–40). He also said, "'For whoever wants to save his life will lose it, but whoever loses his life for me will find it'" (Matt. 16:25).

Throughout Scripture, Christians are exhorted to be concerned with the welfare of others (Matthew 10:42; Luke 9:48). These are powerful motivations if they are implemented in day-to-day family living. Many family disputes are the result of a spiritual problem at this very basic point—namely, one or more family members regard themselves as the first or ultimate priority rather than exhibiting a higher commitment to God and to the welfare of those around them. When spiritual needs like this are identified by the family counselors, they incorporate the problem into their counseling goals with the particular family member or members concerned. Anger at a family member, for example, subjects one to God's judgment

(Matthew 5:21, 22); on the other hand, positive attitudes, coupled with prayer, lead to positive rewards (Matthew 6:5, 6). Christian family counselors express concern not only for the immediate well-being of individual family members, but also for their ultimate spiritual welfare.

The Lord's Prayer

The Christian counselor takes the divine perspective in viewing family problems. Jesus' model prayer, which he offered for his followers, is relevant to the concerns of families in counseling. Jesus instructed them, and us, "This is how you should pray:

"'Our Father in heaven,
hallowed be your name,
your kingdom come
your will be done
　　on earth as it is in heaven.
Give us today our daily bread.
Forgive us our debts,
　　as we also have forgiven our debtors.
And lead us not into temptation,
but deliver us from the evil one.'"

This prayer takes a radically different perspective. Typically, an individual or family group comes to a counselor primarily seeking their own happiness. From a Christian perspective, the pursuit of happiness for its own sake is not a legitimate counseling goal. This prayer offers a different perspective, that of first acknowledging God's existence, lifting up his character of holiness and righteousness, and then praying for his will to be done in our human affairs here on earth as it is in heaven.

Christians then ask for their daily needs. It is significant that the next component of the prayer pertains to the need for forgiveness. So many families who are troubled enough to come to counseling have difficulty forgiving those who have sinned against them. This is not to minimize the pain, the hurt, and the struggle which results when one family member sins against another. This prayer, however, lifts up the necessity to forgive one another.

Forgiveness involves recognizing that there is a cost involved and then consciously choosing to accept that loss. Forgiveness is not saying, "Oh, it doesn't matter, so I forgive you." That is not genuine forgiveness. If the father loans the son $1,000 and then later forgives him of the debt, that means the father is accepting a $1,000 loss. Similarly, God's forgiveness cost him something—separation from his own Son. If we do not forgive family members, it will cost us in another way in terms of the bitterness and resentment that is carried forward from day to day.

Another component of this prayer that is relevant to the family counseling situation is the request, "Lead us not into temptation." Many of the difficulties that families experience relate to the root problem of falling into a temptation repeatedly. Furthermore, in light of the very common practice of American people to turn to God in prayer, this model prayer teaches the crucial importance of taking our problems to God in prayer with the right perspective.

Using the Bible

Even when Christian family counselors are not referring to specific Scripture passages in their work with the family, their overall work of formulating counseling goals is guided by biblical principles. At other times in the family counseling process, the Christian counselor will want to be direct and explicit about bringing to bear Scripture on a family's problem and so he or she may recite a passage from memory or read a portion of God's word to a family and ask family members how it applies to their situation. In yet other situations, the Christian counselor would not be satisfied with simply bringing a biblical passage to the attention of the family, but instead would want to call the family to a decision with regard to the matter addressed in Scripture. An individual family member may need to choose to follow God's commandment. In other cases, the family needs to hear comfort from God's word. On one occasion, a family came in for help in the grieving process because the young wife and mother had died. Certainly, there was nothing the family could do about the mother's death. But it was helpful to hear words of comfort from God's Word and learn how to put that comfort into effect in their family life.

THE BIBLE'S VIEW OF THE FAMILY

O Israel, listen: Jehovah is our God, Jehovah alone. You must love him with *all* your heart, soul and might. And you must think constantly about these commandments I am giving you today. You must teach them to your children and talk about them when you are at home or out for a walk; at bedtime and the first thing in the morning. . . . he has commanded us to obey all of these laws and to reverence him so that he can preserve us alive as he has until now. For it always goes well when we obey all the laws of the Lord our God.   (Deuteronomy 6:4–7, 24–25 TLB)

Many specific commandments about family life are found in the Old and New Testament Scriptures. The Christian family counselor attempts to incorporate all this biblical teaching into the counseling process, and the strategic place where these teachings can be most significant is in the selection of counseling goals. Family cohesiveness, identity, and well-being arise from the sense of order that is derived from an awareness of family heritage, following specific family roles, and participating in the spiritual life of the church.

Jesus' mother had expectations for what Jesus' life would be that were expressed when she and Joseph presented their offerings and brought the child Jesus to the temple where they received a blessing of promise for the child. This passage also teaches that Jesus sat with the elders of the temple and yet he was subject to his parents (Luke 2:22–51). The Hebrew heritage involved a world view in which the home and synagogue supported one another in nurturing the child from young infancy through adolescence. As Jesus developed, there was a balance maintained between the physical, social, psychological, and spiritual aspects of his family life. "And Jesus grew in wisdom, in stature, and in favor with God and man" (Luke 2:52). Participation in the life of the religious community was a very important aspect of the spiritual growth of Jesus, who provides a model for Christian family life.

The biblical model of a family pictures family members as having differing roles, functions, and abilities, but at the same time working together toward the common good. Scripture presents some clear teaching regarding the role of the husband/father and the role of the wife/mother in the family.

The Husband/Father's Role in the Family

Scripture presents a picture of family government by drawing an analogy to Christ and his headship over the church. Scripture teaches that the man is the head of the woman just as Christ is the head of the church, having given himself sacrificially in love for the church's redemption. Similarly, the husband has an obligation to sacrifice unselfishly for the wife and commit himself to her. Looking to Christ as his head for direction, he must actively love his wife in providing for her and in cherishing her (Ephesians 5:22–33; Colossians 3:18, 19; 1 Timothy 3:11, 12; 1 Corinthians 11:3; 14:34, 35; 1 Peter 3:7).

This means that in a family counseling session where the counselor observes the husband exerting his authority over his wife in a dictatorial manner which demeans her dignity as a human being, the counselor has the obligation to bring to that husband's attention this biblical teaching and to urge him to cease his unloving action and follow the biblical pattern.

The Bible gives leadership to the husband such that if a critical matter is in dispute, the marriage relationship should not be seen as a democracy which would have a one-to-one tie vote. Instead, the husband's responsibility is to lovingly make the final decision (Ephesians 5:22–6:4). The husband cannot voluntarily abdicate his headship position in the family in order to evade the responsibilities that are associated with it, according to Paul's teaching. The husband does not need to affirm his right of headship, and he cannot be displaced from this position by the wife unless he is physically or mentally impaired to such a degree that he cannot exercise this responsibility.

The man's authority is a position that is assigned by God, according to Scripture, and therefore any legitimate authority that he has derives from God's order (Romans 13:1; Ephesians 5:22–33). This means that the husband has no legitimate right to order that his wife do something sinful and similarly the wife is not required to obey the husband if his command would require her to disobey God. This places a responsibility on the wife to be well-informed of God's Word, enabled to exercise her own responsibility and moral judgment in following the husband's lead (1 Peter 3:1–6). The biblical pattern affirms that the husband should exercise his headship position in a spirit of love and servanthood, with Jesus as the example (Philippians 2:5–11; Matthew 20:28). The husband has a major responsibility to serve his family (Matthew 20:26), and not "lord it over" his family (Colossians 3:19, 21; Ephesians 6:4). The Christian husband is to have a willingness to sacrifice himself in order to protect his wife and children physically and spiritually (Ephesians 5:25), and therefore the husband has no right from Scripture to attend to his own needs first.

1 Timothy 5:8 and Genesis 3:17–19 teach that a man has a responsibility to provide financial support for his family. Scripture allows the wife to augment the family's income through efficient management and some forms of business (Proverbs 31:10–31). But Scripture does not give the husband a right to force his wife to abandon her calling in the home for the purpose of material gain (1 Timothy 5:8; Ephesians 5:5). It is not legitimate for a Christian husband to push his wife to work outside the home for the mere acquisition of a higher standard of living or a middle-class lifestyle (1 Timothy 6:8). A husband should carefully analyze his motives for desiring his wife to work outside the home to insure that materialistic motives are not overshadowing the spiritual responsibilities of child-rearing.

The family counselor will observe that some husbands use their need to provide materially for the family as a rationalization for their failure to provide spiritual guidance for their wife and children. Biblical principles would exhort the Christian husband not to do this (1 Timothy 3:4; 1 Peter 3:7; Ephesians 5:28, 29).

To the contrary, Scripture teaches that the Christian man should lead his children in the way of godliness by constant teaching, by living the Christian life as an example, and by leading the family in worship (Deuteronomy 6:7; 11:19; Ephesians 6:4; Psalm 34:11; 78:5, 6). The Christian father and husband has the responsibility of protecting his family. This includes praying for the protection of his family and asking for God's blessing on them in regular prayer (1 Timothy 2:8; 1 Thessalonians 5:17; 1 Peter 3:7); he should not presume on God to protect his family without actively seeking God's help (James 4:2). The Bible teaches that in many ways God treats the family as a whole, as a household under a man who is the head (Acts 16:31; John 4:53; Acts 11:14) and in cases where the Christian husband and father is not present, the woman assumes the leadership responsibility with God's assistance (for example, Lydia in Acts 16:14, 15, and Lois and Eunice in 2 Timothy 1:5, see Acts 16:1).

The Wife/Mother's Role in the Family

Scripture uses the analogy of the church under submission to Christ as a picture of how the wife is called by God to willingly submit in love and in obedience to her husband (Ephesians 5:22–24; Colossians 3:18). Scripture does not teach that the wife should submit to anything demanded by the husband that is contrary to God's will (2 Peter 3:6); nor does it teach that the Christian wife cannot respectfully rebuke her Christian husband as his sister in the Lord (Ephesians 5:21; Colossians 3:16), but that it is something she should do in a gentle and respectful way, without badgering the husband with constant criticism (2 Peter 3:1–5).

The Bible pictures the woman's primary duty as that of bearing and nurturing her children, being busy managing the home, and making the home productive economically and as a center for ministry (1 Timothy 5:10, 14; Titus 2:4, 5; Proverbs 31:10–31). She should see this as a fulfilling calling of God, and she need not capitulate to the common cultural notion in America that work is not valuable unless it has a salary attached to it. This kind of materialistic evaluation is contrary to biblical teaching. A woman need not seek her identity or worth in income production outside the home but instead should reject the world's idea of self-fulfillment and pursue her calling from God (Matthew 16:24–26; Mark 8:34, 35; Luke 9:23–26).

How These Biblical Teachings Apply to the Formation of Counseling Goals

When the Christian counselor deals with a Christian family that accepts the authority of Scripture, it is not as difficult to set some goals for family counseling. The counselor and the family who share the same value orientation will find it easier to come to terms with how biblical principles apply to their family situation. But in families in which a Christian family member is living together with a nonbeliever, there may be considerable conflict when it comes to setting goals. The nonbeliever may be vocally opposed to biblical values and may insist that the counselor be "value free" in the counseling approach. Unfortunately, the research evidence indicates that even when values are not explicitly talked about in counseling, after a few sessions the counselee has begun to shift his or her values to match the values of the counselor. Therefore, there are some indirect ways in which the counselor inevitably communicates his or her values to the counselee. Counseling, by its very nature, is a value-laden endeavor. Setting any goal for counseling involves making a value judgment as to what goal is chosen and what goal is not.

When there is difficulty in establishing goals, the general rule would be to try to deal with the problems that family members bring in as their problem and to begin at their level. Try to seek some common ground. Find out where you as the counselor share some value in common with the Christian family member and the non-Christian.

The McAndrews family was a challenge for a Christian counselor because the wife was a believer but the husband was quite resistant to principles drawn from Scripture. Mrs. McAndrews insisted, "I believe my husband should be the leader in our family." But he was obviously a very passive person who rejected the biblical model of headship. He would reply, "No, I want my wife to take charge of the children. After all, I am so busy with my demanding work, and I am extremely tired when I get home. I don't want to be that involved with the kids' lives." Mr. and Mrs. McAndrews had a history of considerable conflict between themselves regarding who should discipline the children and over the issue of how involved Mr. McAndrews should or should not be.

Now ideally, both with respect to the researched effects of fathering on child development and with regard to the biblical model, it would be desirable for Mr. McAndrews to become a Christian and follow the role of the true spiritual leader in his family. But at the moment, he was not at all interested in spiritual things. In fact, he was extremely emotional about his rejection of Christianity. To press the issue would risk bringing on a divorce, which he threatened from time to time.

In this case, Mrs. McAndrews had become a Christian after she was married, and neither she nor her husband had the biblical model in mind for child-rearing when they first got married. Therefore the biblical admonition would be for this wife to attempt to win her husband over by a quiet and gentle respect and submission to his desire insofar as that is possible. Her responsibilities would be to pray for his spiritual well-being and to do the best she can in nurturing the children spiritually.

Mr. McAndrews had a quite violent temper. In the first counseling session, he yelled, "I'm not Mr. Perfect. Sure, I've had a number of affairs, not that I'm bragging about it. She knows about it, so she knows I'm not Mr. Perfect. But after all, we do have these children and I'm providing for them, what more does she expect?"

For this family, establishing a goal took more time and was a difficult process. The Christian counselor could resonate with the father in terms of his provision of the material needs of his wife and children. It is important to identify the strengths of the family members and try to build upon those strengths. It was unwise for the wife to precipitate arguments, particularly in light of Mr. McAndrews's tendency to lose his temper and to explode. He even blurted out in the first session, "Sure, I get angry and lose my temper, and I'm not saying that I don't rough her up a bit from time to time."

In a case like this, a counselor needs to initially set a few short-term goals and to get started somewhere. Working with the husband on containing his physical violence would be an urgent priority. The counselor should certainly inquire about his treatment of the children. To explore aspects of the family relationship that precipitate his angry outbursts and to help him learn self-control would be helpful not only to him but to the entire family.

With this non-Christian husband, it would not be wise for the Christian counselor to quote chapter and verse. If an individual has overt hostility to the Bible, this approach fails. This does not mean that the Christian counselor is not following biblical principles in making recommendations to the family, but it is wise to first build a positive relationship and maintain rapport before gently exploring some of the spiritual issues with this husband.

PARENTS AND THEIR CHILDREN

A very common goal in family counseling is to strengthen the parental coalition between the mother and father so they can work together more effectively as a team in their child-rearing responsibilities. If parents have become disengaged from one another, they are not able to work in a mutually supportive way in disciplining and nurturing the children. Therefore, the family counselor often needs to facilitate greater family intimacy and cooperation.

For a Christian family counselor, this is based upon the scriptural teaching that children are indeed a blessing from God. Children are of great worth which is even beyond our human capacity to measure, and parents should welcome them into the family as a gift from the Creator. Children do not belong to the parents but instead to God alone, with the parents being their God-appointed stewards. The Bible teaches that parents have the primary responsibility and authority for educating the children and providing for their physical and spiritual well-being (Genesis 33:5; Psalm 78:1–8; 127:3–5; Proverbs 17:6; Ephesians 6:1–4; 1 Timothy 2:15; Deuteronomy 4:9; 6:1–9).

Parents, reflecting the image of God, should mirror the divine characteristics of love, justice, mercy, and righteousness in their role of disciplining, training, and nurturing children

(Proverbs 22:6; 29:15; 1 Samuel 3:13; Psalm 78:1–8; 2 Timo-thy 1:5; 3:15; Ephesians 6:1–4; 2 Corinthians 12:14). Children are to honor and obey their parents in the Lord and parents have a responsibility to enforce obedience through lovingly ad-ministered discipline, which may include corporal punishment (Deuteronomy 5:16; 2 Samuel 7:14; see Proverbs 3:11, 12; Proverbs 13:24; 22:15; 23:13; 29:15). The Bible teaches that an overarching goal of parenthood should be to present the children to God as spiritually mature adults by the time they reach physical maturity, and in this regard, teenagers are viewed as responsible individuals undergoing something like an apprenticeship for adulthood (Luke 2:41, 42).

Both the children and the parents need to recognize that a family is not a democracy where each family member has an equal vote. This does not mean that parents cannot listen care-fully to what their children or adolescents might propose in terms of family rules, but everyone in the family should recognize the parents' authority to set the final rules for the children.

One area of considerable conflict between teenagers and their parents has to do with family rules regarding getting home at night by a certain hour and keeping the parents in-formed as to where a teenager is. If Tim tells his mother he's going to John's house to shoot baskets and if he arrives at John's house, indeed shoots a few baskets, but decides to go with John to get a hamburger, the parents may want to en-force some kind of rule for Tim on keeping them posted as to where he is.

If there's a lot of conflict over what the adolescent allegedly knew and did not know about what the rules were, the family counselor may want to negotiate an agreement between the parents with the input of the adolescent and put the agree-ment in writing. Then each family member can sign the agreement, copies can be made for each person, and a copy can be left with the counselor. This way, there is no ambiguity about exactly what the expectations of the parents are and what the consequences are if the expectations are not ful-filled. A behavioral contract of this sort may fulfill the goal of having clear communication between parents and youngsters with regard to behavioral expectations which the parents have authority to set.

In formulating goals while counseling families, the counselor should keep in mind that parents have a tremendous influence on the lives of their children, and indirectly a historically significant responsibility for succeeding generations. The parents' style of leadership in the family will have consequences not only in the present but also in the future because the results of righteous living and the results of sinful living affect succeeding generations through one's children. Christian parents may turn to family counseling to assist them in providing for their children a more biblical approach to family life than they themselves had experienced when they grew up, and this overarching goal, if achieved, will help promote the nurturance and growth of the church for generations. The biblical principles regarding the historical significance of each family can be found in Exodus 20:5; Deuteronomy 5:9, 10, 16; Jeremiah 35:18, 19; Lamentations 5:7; Psalm 78:1–8; and Acts 2:39. The Bible teaches that the family's relationship to God exists over time down through generations and that some effects of God's promises reach down to the third and fourth generations. Many promises of spiritual life are given to an individual and his household (see also Genesis 12:2, 3; Acts 16:31; 1 Corinthians 7:14; 1 Timothy 5:3–16; 2 Timothy 1:5).

Single adults are not neglected in the biblical view of the family, even though they do not immediately experience the possibility of having effects of their lives cross generations over time through rearing children. God calls some individuals to singlehood instead of marriage, and single adults should invest their time with single-minded zeal for God's kingdom (1 Corinthians 7:32, 34; Ecclesiastes, 12:1–7). This means that singleness through adulthood is not viewed as an extended childhood in which one can pursue selfish endeavors and indulge in sexual immorality. Rather the whole of scriptural teaching would include singles within their own extended family networks and in close relationship with other families in the church (Psalm 68 and Romans 6).

Considering these teachings from Scripture, we see that the

family who approaches life from a biblical world view, as well as the Christian engaged in counseling families, would hold to a number of central values that would undergird the whole purpose of family counseling. The goals negotiated for the process of family counseling would derive from these biblical values which would include, for example:

1. A firm commitment to the institution of marriage and its intended permanence,
2. The belief in the desirability of children and in the primary responsibility of parents for their own children,
3. The sanctity of all human life (whether handicapped, sick, unborn, young, or old),
4. The desirability of having stable and harmonious family relationships as opposed to chaotic family relationships,
5. The importance of effective child-rearing techniques for promoting proper spiritual, emotional, social, and physical development, and
6. The value of passing on cultural values from one generation to another through the family.

As a central unit in society, the family's preservation is not only crucial for individual well-being but also for social stability. Inherent in most family counseling is a set of moral values that endorses the continuance of the family way of life as opposed to a self-centered orientation focused upon individual "rights."

CHAPTER FOUR

GOALS OF FAMILY COUNSELING

A COUNSELOR WILL HAVE a number of broad therapeutic goals for families. These general goals, for the Christian, derive from the biblical concept of love that includes nurturing, helping, caring, supporting, comforting, and physical affection (see for example 1 Corinthians 13). Both the Christian family and the Christian counselor would believe that family members should love one another and that this love is to be evident in the way in which they forgive one another, tenderly help one another, support one another in tangible ways, protect one another, and comfort one another. Rather than taking family members for granted or withholding needed love from them, Christians expect that individual family members should be regularly expressing affection toward one another as well as mutual respect.[1] This overarching biblical concept of love can be translated into a number of general goals for family counseling.

ENHANCING EFFECTIVE COMMUNICATION

When family members are effectively loving one another, there will be simple, fair, straightforward communication of each person's needs, feelings, and ideas within the family circle. A goal of family counseling is to increase effective communication where a family has deficits in this regard. Communication, of course, involves not only the practice of individual members expressing their needs, feelings, and thoughts to one another but also the regular practice of listening to one another within the family. Love is expressed when the family members care enough to take the time to listen carefully to one another. Often the family counselor needs to teach listening skills as well as skills in communicating thoughts and emotions.

All too often, families who come for counseling have a pattern of negative criticism repeated back and forth. Because individuals tend to reciprocate the type of communication they receive (theologians would describe this as a sinful pattern [Romans 12:17]), the use of criticism is not the most effective way to handle conflicts in family relationships. In fact, criticism is often counterproductive.

The Bible teaches that being critical and holding grudges will destroy the spiritual harmony between a person and God (Ephesians 4:26, 31; Colossians 3:8). Criticism also inhibits growth in individuals and harmony in family life. This damage affects the individual doing the harsh judging as well as the person being judged. Matthew 5:23 and 24 teach, "Therefore, if you are offering your gift at the altar and there remember that your brother has something against you, leave your gift there in front of the altar. First go and be reconciled with your brother; then come and offer your gift." Luke 6:37 and 38 teach, "Do not judge, and you will not be judged. Do not condemn, and you will not be condemned. Forgive and you will be forgiven. Give, and it will be given to you. . . . For with the measure you use, it will be measured to you." The Bible teaches that individuals should "turn the other cheek" (Matthew 5:39–48) instead of dealing with conflict with harsh criticism and physical force and that they should "do to others as you would have them do to you" (Luke 6:31).

In a family in which there is repeated criticism, the family counselor seeks to increase positive interaction between family members and to decrease the harmful criticism. The goal may be to help family members express appreciation for one another. The book of Acts tells of a man named Joseph who was nicknamed Barnabas by the Christians because he encouraged others.[2] Criticism should be replaced with encouraging and loving remarks among family members.

MODIFYING DISTURBED, INFLEXIBLE PATTERNS AND COALITIONS

When two or more members in the family system team up against other family members, an unhealthy coalition is formed. We described this kind of problem in chapter 2. From a biblical point of view, the Christian counselor would see this pattern as being displeasing to God in addition to being painful for some family members. Scripture teaches that human beings are made in God's image and that through Jesus Christ individuals can share a oneness with God in the Spirit (Genesis 1:26; John 17:11, 21–23). Furthermore, members in a family may experience a unity, a oneness with one another and with God in the Spirit, which is appropriated through faith in Jesus Christ. What the Bible describes is a unity within the family with God which in turn strengthens the cohesiveness of the family. On the one hand, there is a healthy sense of individuality in which each family member is responsible for his or her behavior before God. But in addition, God was the Creator of the family unit and he intended a corporate oneness which reflects the pattern of individuality as well as unity in the three persons of the Godhead—Father, Son, and Holy Spirit. The Bible teaches that within the Trinity there is perfect love and communication. In that we are created in God's image, human beings living within a family unit are intended to express love and communication in their family life, and this is made possible through the presence of the Holy Spirit in regenerated family members.

In contrast, when a family experiences the disturbed and inflexible patterns of coalitions of two or more family members against other family members, there is a situation that has been created by sin which, in turn, is a result of the Fall (Genesis 3). Many times the family counselor can trace the history of how family members have been sinned against by previous family members down through the generations. The Christian family counselor, therefore, has as a goal the replacing of these disturbed coalitions with a loving and mutual submission among family members. In the Bible's teaching of submission in relationships, we have the idea of an autonomous individual deliberately choosing to defer his or her own personal self-interest in order to attend first to the interest of the other family members. Of course the motivation behind submission is love and concern for the well-being of family members. Individual family members derive their capacity for being submissive to others in the family by first experiencing God's perfect love and forgiveness and then responding to that love by obeying Jesus' commandment to love one another (Matthew 5:44–46; 19:19; 22:37–39).[3] Submission, therefore, works for the good of all members within the family and it generates a kind of freedom for the one who has submitted as well as for the one submitted to.

OVERCOMING ENMESHMENT

Emotional problems, spiritual problems, and relationship problems of individuals can be interlocked with family problems. One example of this is the problem of enmeshment, which we discussed in chapter 2. When a counselor observes enmeshment in a family, the goal is to help differentiate individual family members from the family unit. Some families have developed an enmeshed pattern in which individuality is simply not tolerated and artificial sameness is imposed in abnormally close and entangled family relationships.

This pattern was observed in Greg's family. As an eight-year-old, Greg had a very difficult time deciding what he would wear in the morning. His mother was so involved with every little detail of his life that he developed little sense of his own individuality and little sense of the possibility of making his own choices. Greg would look in his closet and see a blue shirt, a green shirt, and a yellow shirt, but his mother would not allow him to pick which one to wear. Instead, she arbitrarily imposed her own choice by dictating, "Today you should wear the blue one."

Later, as a fifteen-year-old, Greg was still not allowed any independent decision-making. His mother told him exactly when to take a shower. She even insisted, "This time make sure you shampoo, rinse your hair, and use soap on your whole body." Greg's mother had developed an unhealthy and excessive overinvolvement with her son. In dealing with these enmeshed patterns, the counselor needs to clarify why enmeshment is a problem and set out to develop healthy individuality in family members.

Other counselors attempt to untangle family enmeshment by establishing clear boundaries between the members. In the Wade family (described in chapter 2) it was not quite clear who was behaving as the parent and who was behaving as the child. This family lacked clear boundaries between the parents' role and the child's role. So, establishing clear boundaries is often a goal in counseling families. The Bible teaches principles regarding the father's leadership and authority in a family and the obligation of the children to obey their parents. When properly put into practice, these biblical principles can establish clear and appropriate boundaries.

CORRECTING EXCESSIVE INDIVIDUALISM

While some families have too much controlling togetherness, other families are composed of individualistic members who are quite remote from one another. C. S. Lewis once observed that sin comes in opposite pairs and Satan delights to see someone avoid one extreme only to sin by backing into the opposite pitfall. If you could picture enmeshment as two circles right on top of one another, excessive individualism could be pictured as two circles completely apart from one another. The balance to achieve in family life would be overlapping circles which still have some unique space of their own.

Some families maintain a veneer of adjustment by avoiding all close contact which could lead to potential conflict. In such a family, the counselor's goal would be to develop true mutuality. Many families keep up a convincing appearance of unity but lack meaningful relationships. Their unity is based on the avoidance of dealing with the issues and conflicts rather than on a true mutuality of working together and being highly committed to one another.

RESOLVING CONFLICT THROUGH FORGIVENESS AND RECONCILIATION

Have you ever noticed the tendency that we all have to greet strangers or guests in our home with more courtesy than we typically give to our family members? An extension of this tendency leads family members to behave self-righteously and deliberately withhold forgiveness from one another, a cruelty that they would never think of inflicting on strangers, guests, or people at work. The teachings of the Bible exhort Christians to have the same level of self-control and courtesy at home as they would have in the world outside.

The Bible affirms that all people are fallen, imperfect and sinful and in desperate need of forgiveness and redemption by God.[4] Furthermore, because every human being is sinful, it is inevitable that this sin will eventually be expressed toward fellow family members and thereby require forgiveness and reconciliation to restore normal healthy family life.

The Christian counselor, guided by the Holy Spirit, has a role in encouraging reconciliation among family members. The application of the Bible's teaching on reconciliation can be the basis for resolving family conflicts. The biblical concept includes forgiving one another, refraining from holding grudges, and loving one another. From this basis, Christian family members are able to resolve conflict and on a daily basis show the same level of courtesy to family members that they would show to a guest in their home (James 2:8, 9).

The Bible teaches that *the* fundamental human need is to be in a reconciled relationship with God and thereby have peace with God. Jesus Christ alone is able to offer this gift of peace. This peace with God carries with it a profound impact upon family life with all its problems, troubles, and conflicts.

Rejoice in the Lord always. I will say it again: Rejoice! Let your gentleness be evident to all. The Lord is near. Do not be anxious about anything, but in everything, by prayer and petition, with thanksgiving, present your request to God. And the *peace of God,* which transcends all understanding, will guard your hearts and your minds in Christ Jesus.   (Phil. 4:4–7)

If the fundamental human need is to be in a reconciled relationship with God, and if the conflict and separations among family members can be ultimately traced back to their separation from God, then genuine unity among family members can never be permanently accomplished apart from the gospel of Jesus Christ. If we fully appreciate the ultimate cause for conflict and division among people, then the biblical world view would teach us that genuine and lasting reconciliation is only possible through the power of Jesus Christ's work through the Holy Spirit.

Furthermore, the biblical teaching on reconciliation directly implies a distinction between superficial unity and genuine reconciliation among family members. Often a parent and child or a husband and wife appear to have a harmonious relationship of cooperation and freedom from overt conflict. Special circumstances may bring people together to work on a shared project. But time is the test as to whether the unity is genuine or superficial. Marriages based upon superficial unity unravel, sooner or later, into conflict, separation, and in too many cases, divorce. Parent-child relationships based on superficial unity similarly can unravel under pressure.

A Reconciled Relationship with God

Because the process of reconciliation is so central to Christian family counseling, it is essential to outline the biblical doctrine of reconciliation beginning with Paul's teaching in 2 Corinthians 5:17–19:

Therefore, if anyone is in Christ, he is a new creation: the old has gone, the new has come! All this is from *God, who reconciled us to himself* through Christ and gave us the ministry of reconciliation: that *God was reconciling the world to himself* in Christ, not counting men's sins against them. And he has committed to us the message of reconciliation (italics added).

This Scripture passage teaches that the atonement was primarily intended to reconcile God to the sinner. It is also true that Scripture refers to the sinner's being reconciled to God (Romans 5:10; 2 Corinthians 5:19, 20), but this should be understood as the secondary and subjective side of reconciliation. God, as the offended party, reconciles us (the offenders) to himself by not counting our sins against us. This is not the result of any moral change in us, but instead is based in the fact that the death of Christ has met the demands of the law to satisfy God for the believer. This is clarified in Romans 5:10, 11:

For if, when we were God's enemies, we were reconciled to him through the death of his Son, how much more, having been reconciled, shall we be saved through his life! Not only is this so, but we also rejoice in God through our Lord Jesus Christ, through whom we have now received reconciliation.

Romans 5 emphasizes God's power in salvation to affect the human condition in very personal and relational terms. Later chapters in Romans teach us what it means to be a member of the new family of God, what the Holy Spirit's power brings to that relationship, what it means to have a likeness to the image of Christ, and how reconciliation unfolds in our relationships with other people.

This reconciliation was necessary because of the estrangement sin caused between God and humanity. Reconciliation repairs this total breach, eliminates the war between God and humanity, and saves the individual from the terrible plight of being a doomed enemy of an all-powerful God. Without peace with God, individuals are without hope. They are trapped in sin and rebellion and literally powerless to help themselves in this moral dilemma. "Peace with God" is not a mere feeling of inner tranquility, but it is the objective result of being in a restored relationship of acceptance with God based upon salvation from the wrath of God in the day of judgment (see Romans 5:9).

Reconciled Relationships with Others

The reconciliation experienced by the believer should result in peaceful relationships with others: "Let us therefore make every effort to do what leads to peace and to mutual edification" (Rom. 14:19). Furthermore, Colossians 3:15 reads, "Let the peace of Christ rule in your hearts, since as members of one body you are called to peace . . . ." This link between the concepts of reconciliation and unity with fellow humans is further developed in Ephesians 2:11–22. The core of this truth is stated in verses 13–16:

> But now in Christ Jesus you who once were far away have been brought near through the blood of Christ. For he himself is our peace, who has made the two one and has destroyed the barrier, the dividing wall of hostility, by abolishing in his flesh the law with its commandments and regulations. His purpose was to create in himself one new man out of the two, thus making peace, and in this one body to reconcile both of them to God through the cross, by which he put to death their hostility.

This passage extends the teaching regarding reconciliation between God and humanity to a proclamation of Christ's redeeming work of uniting hostile individuals by removing the offensive factor that kept them apart. When two individuals at odds with one another each become individually reconciled to God, they also experience the means of being likewise reconciled to one another. In the language of verse 19, they become "fellow citizens."

One important implication of Ephesians 2:11, 12 is that sin not only separates human beings from God but separates one person from another. Verse 14 of the same passage implies that sin puts humans at enmity with one another as well as with God. The sin of pride, the sin of setting oneself up as autonomous from God's moral requirements, was the sin of Adam and Eve in response to Satan's temptation (Genesis 3:1). From the position of pride and self-centeredness, the psychological results of rivalry, jealousy, envy, coveting, competition, and conflict between humans inevitably emerge, as they did in the first human family.

In this context, it is instructive that when Jesus answered the Pharisees' question, "Which is the greatest commandment in the Law?" he said, "'Love the Lord your God with all your heart and with all your soul and with all your mind.' This is the first and greatest commandment. And the second is like it: 'Love your neighbor as yourself'" (Matthew 22:37–39). The right relationship with God precedes right relationships between people. As Lord and Savior, Jesus Christ brings not only peace with God but also peace among individuals.

Reconciled Relationships with Family Members

Ephesians 2 describes how enmity results between people as a result of sin. In a family, this sinful pattern can occur like this: God gives a particular gift to one family member—such as a quick ability to understand—and in sin, this person becomes proud in looking at his brother, "Who is he? What does he know? He doesn't understand—he's stupid." Instead of jointly thanking God for such a gift, the two persons become ensnarled with the correlates of this sin—jealousy, rivalry, hatred, bitterness, scorn, and enmity.

The good news is that Christ's purpose was ". . . to reconcile both of them to God through the cross, by which he put to death their hostility" (Ephesians 2:16). This passage implies that the divisions, quarrels, and separations between human beings in the family and outside the family can be ultimately traced back to the basic cause of one or the other being separated from God. The lack of genuine love among family members can be attributed to a lack of fellowship with God, who is the author of love. The restoration of unity among individuals therefore requires reconciliation together to God—the secondary effect of Christ's reconciling God to us.

The regenerated family members are exhorted to be imitators of God and to walk in love (2 Corinthians 6:18; Ephesians 5:1, 2). This means that reconciliation of the believer to God in the vertical relationship then has implications for the horizontal

97

relationships in family life. Jesus' parable of the Prodigal Son is a human analogy to the reconciliation possible between God and man (Luke 15:11–32). The Bible teaches that the steps of reconciliation move from reconciliation of ourselves to God, to reconciliation within ourselves, to reconciliation with others. Matthew 18:15–18 has further teaching on how reconciliation should work among believers.

CONCLUSION

The values of the family and the values of the family counselor are involved in setting goals for family counseling. The family on the one hand and the counselor on the other hand have certain beliefs regarding what is "good family life." The counselor generally starts with what the family labels as the problem, analyzes the underlying family dynamics, and follows scriptural principles to negotiate counseling goals with the family.

CHAPTER FIVE

WELLNESS AND FAMILY COUNSELING

DAN COATS is the ranking minority member of the Select Committee for Children, Youth, and Families in the United States House of Representatives. As part of his work on that committee, he visited a juvenile detention facility in Santa Ana, California. This facility, considered one of the most modern in the country, was designed on the basis of the latest research. Huge sums of money are spent yearly on staff salaries and operating costs. Yet Congressman Coats described his review of that facility in these words:

> About fifty young people were incarcerated there and participating in the program. While there, we had time to

speak individually with the counselors and the children. I came away with almost a sense of despair because here we had the very best of facilities that money could buy, the best of techniques, yet there didn't seem to be any progress. There didn't seem to be any hope present in the lives of the people we spoke with.

As I talked to one of the counselors afterward, I said, "You have kids here with delinquent behavior, drug, drinking and sex problems, and all the other problems that are common to young people today. If you could boil all this down, what is the common cause? What is the lowest common denominator? What is the one reason these kids are in this place?"

He very quickly replied, "Well, I've been involved in this work for twenty-five years and I've spent a lot of time asking that same question. The one common denominator is that every one of the kids in this facility is from what I would call a disoriented family. There is something present in the family that is out of sync. It is not what we would call normal—if there is something such as a normal family. The kids here who are violent have been subject to violence in their families. The kids here who are on drugs or drinking have seen drug abuse in their family. We see this cycle being repeated and repeated."[1]

Every family counselor knows the devastating effect that problem families can have on adults and children alike. Nick Stinnett, one of the leading researchers in the area of family strengths, pinpointed the key issue: "Many of our major social problems—juvenile delinquency, child abuse, spouse abuse, elder abuse, some forms of mental illness—can be linked very closely to bad quality of family life, that is, to the absence of family strengths. I think each of us knows deep inside that so much of our happiness, so much of our emotional well-being depends or is influenced to a great degree by the quality of the human relationships we have, and particularly by the quality of those intimate relationships we call family relationships. So promoting family strengths should be one of our country's top priorities."[2]

Certainly the family is the cradle of any culture. The family is a basic unit in society for nurturing human development. From a Christian perspective, the family is a basic unit for worshiping God, for making disciples, for evangelism and for other ministries of help and hospitality to others.

The overarching goal of family counseling should be to promote family wellness. This goes beyond merely helping the family solve its problems, conflicts, and malfunctioning.

At a meeting of the N.A.E. (National Association of Evangelicals) Task Force on the Family, we were focusing on the topic of broken families—families broken by divorce and runaway children. One of the task force members suggested, "We need to review the results of research on the causes of family breakup so we can advise churches on how to specifically operate programs to prevent divorce and other forms of family breakup." At that time, I was the head of the Department of Family and Child Development at Kansas State University, and so naturally the task force members turned to me for some statement regarding the availability of research on preventing family breakups. While I agreed that it would be useful for the task force to review such research, I proposed that the task force also develop a model of family wellness based upon the research on positive family models. I raised the question, what are the characteristics of strong families which are not breaking up?

Nick Stinnett insists that this is the crux of the issue.

I would not dream of teaching someone how to play tennis by only telling them how *not* to do it: "Now you do *not* hold the racket this way. You do *not* do a back stroke this way." A coach would not succeed if he only made remarks like, "This is wrong, don't stand like this, this is terrible," while never telling the person how to stand right and how to hold the tennis racket correctly. But, unfortunately, to a large extent we have done that in the area of family life. For example, we've told people what the families of delinquents or runaways are like, and we've said, "Now, don't let your family be like that." We have not used the positive model approach. We have not said, "Here's what a strong family is like and your family can work on these positive qualities."[3]

It is extremely useful and perhaps mandatory that every family counselor have clearly in mind a model of a well-functioning family. Studies published by a number of researchers in recent years now make it possible for us to report on the characteristics that strong, healthy, adaptive families have in common.[4] For example, Dr. Stinnett and his colleagues studied over three thousand families who rated themselves very high in terms of marriage happiness and in terms of their satisfaction in parent-child relationships.[5] Other people in the community endorsed these families as examples of healthy family functioning. After extensive study of these families through questionnaires, interviewing, and following protocol of data gathering, the researchers found that these families (from North America, South America, Switzerland, Austria, Germany, and South Africa) had six major qualities in common.

It was found that strong families (1) are committed to the family, (2) spend time together, (3) have good family communication, (4) express appreciation to each other, (5) have a spiritual commitment, and (6) are able to solve problems in a crisis. These six qualities can serve as the positive goals to achieve through family counseling.

COMMITMENT TO FAMILY

Strong families are highly committed to one another and to their family group. Because commitment is often absent in families that seek counseling, the family counselor needs to be able to define this desirable quality so that the family can begin to grasp what it would mean to have a high degree of commitment to one another.

In strong families, family members are determined to promote each other's welfare and they know they have one another's support. This commitment is measured by the high priority they place on family issues and family life. As Stinnett points out, "Commitment is something that is essential to the success of any group—whether it's a football team, a business organization or a family."[6]

This statement reminds me of a conversation I had with one of my university students after class one day. Ron was a business major who took my class, Family Relationships, as an elective. After a lecture in which I had read this quotation on family commitment, Ron came up to the lectern in that large lecture hall and asked if he could ask a question about competing commitments. "I agree that the same level of commitment that is required for success in sports or business is also required for family success, but how can a man balance the demands of family and work which both require high levels of commitment? How do you set priorities?"

We chatted in a theoretical sort of way about how a person can "work smart" instead of overworking by doing the strategic necessities and leaving some challenges to co-workers on a team. When I commented that sometimes hard choices had to be made where a person decides against advancing in a career when it sacrifices family life, Ron's question shifted from the academic to the personal as he poured out his own story.

"My dad was a university football coach and my mom worked full-time as an R.N. in the hospital. Especially during football season, I hardly ever saw my dad. My two sisters were older than I and were in high school and had their own circle of friends. My oldest sister, Brenda, was in charge of looking after me and my younger sister after school and in the evening while Mom was on her nursing shifts. I heard Mom say one time that she was glad when we kids were all school-age, because she knew we didn't need her at home anymore. When she was home, she was running around trying to get all the housework done.

"Brenda's baby-sitting me didn't make up for the father I needed. I didn't adjust well, and began to associate with the wrong crowd. My parents weren't home enough to realize that I had joined a city gang. With Mom and Dad gone so much, we kids just drifted in our own directions with our own friends, and Brenda didn't realize what I was doing either."

Tears welled up in Ron's eyes as he admitted, "I ended up doing some things with that gang that I regret now. I didn't even want to be with my family anymore. I realized that Dad looked down on me for not playing football when I got to high school, and I resented him for it because I felt he had given up on me and that he didn't really care.

"When I was arrested and jailed for criminal activity, my parents found out with a jolt that I was involved with a gang. I'll never forget my dad's shocked look of disbelief when he came down to the police station to bail me out. I guess that shook him up badly, because he totally reorganized his life. He took a leave of absence from coaching, got a less time-demanding teaching job, and decided to make up for the lost time with his family. Mom cut back her work to part-time nursing in a doctor's office. They took us on weekend camping trips and other Saturday trips three times a month. They went with us to church on Sundays, and that's when I turned my life over to Jesus Christ as my Lord and Savior. Even at that late date in our family life, we developed deep bonds of family relationships which were sorely missing before. I experienced the difference between a strong family commitment and the lack of any real commitment to family life."

A high level of family commitment begins typically in the married couple's relationship, where the husband and wife view their solemn vow of marriage as a lifelong commitment to one another "for better or worse." As Nicholi has pointed out, "Commitment involves many things. It involves the interrelationship between child and adult that is extremely complex. It involves identification of the child with the parent. It involves all the kinds of interactions that we understand are necessary in order for the child to develop into a mature human being. But little of that complex process can take place unless the parent is there physically and emotionally, and unless the parent makes a commitment of time."[7]

What starts out as a commitment to the marriage relationship therefore extends to a family commitment in the parent-child relationship after children are born or adopted. In family counseling, it is often necessary to help family members sort out their priorities and see what commitments of time and energy are superseding their commitment to the family.

SPENDING TIME TOGETHER

Closely related to family commitment, the second major characteristic of a strong family is that they spend a great deal of time with one another. When researchers have asked people to identify the happiest memories they have of their family life during childhood, the majority of their reports represent examples of simply doing things together with family members.[8] People recall trips to visit grandparents, working together on projects with the family, playing games with family members, Christmas celebrations with the family, and outdoor camping activities. The kinds of things people recall typically do not require large investments of money, but instead represent major investments in time. Strong families deliberately arrange to spend large amounts of time relating with one another. By contrast, so many problem families have only superficial contact with one another which does not allow for deep and effectual human relationships.

In a written class assignment, a sophomore student of mine described a family in which this important characteristic of "spending time together" was chronically absent. The mother, Evelyn, was a full-time homemaker who was also extensively involved in several women's clubs, one of which had multiple fund-raising drives for charities. The father, Rick, worked on a commission basis for a national distributor of plastic materials and was one of their leading employees for volume of sales. Their sixteen-year-old daughter, Julia, was a junior in high school. Jeff, their thirteen-year-old, was an eighth grader, and Laura was an eleven-year-old in the sixth grade.

Rick's work schedule and short business trips meant that he was rarely home for dinner. When he did come home to eat, he rushed off afterward to work on client accounts, play racquetball, attend choir rehearsal, or attend a church or civic club meeting.

Julia kept a hectic pace with Girl Scouts, church youth group, cheerleading squad, youth choir and after-school French Club. Jeff played on the school tennis team, often stayed late at school for the debate team, and had an active circle of friends. Young Laura participated in an after-school scout troop, flute lessons, junior choir at church, and the "Y" soccer team.

Evelyn was one of the scout leaders for Laura's troop, taught a junior girls' Sunday School class, and was active in the Women's Missionary Society at church, in addition to her community women's club activities. Sandwiched in between all that, she was the "official taxi driver" for the family, transporting them from one activity to another.

The family rarely ate meals together. Each grabbed something for breakfast and ate dinner in shifts in the evening, since their schedule of activities did not match. Evelyn was quite adept at having things available that could be quickly warmed up in the microwave. Family members developed the habit of bringing books and magazines to the table while eating, or eating in front of the TV, so even when two or more were eating at the same time, they rarely talked with each other, except to explain what food was available.

Family members felt "locked" into their schedules. After all, every activity seemed important and worthwhile. The breathless pace might have continued indefinitely if Laura had not happened to spy her dad in the kitchen one day and tearfully and timidly approached him with the words, "I think I need a hug." She then broke down and cried, "I need a family that cares for me."

My student described this family as "an organized activity trap." Even on Sunday morning, everyone was going in a different direction at church, and they did not sit together as a family during the worship service.

At the dad's insistence, this family came to family counseling—not an easy scheduling task. The counselor helped them assess their family life, their needs, and their schedule of activity. He explained how strong families spontaneously hold periodic meetings to list all their activities, evaluate them, and cut out some good activities for a while to permit more time with the family as a unit.

With counseling, this family set new priorities, the father developed leadership skills, and each family member eliminated at least one activity so that the family could eat dinner together and devote one evening a week to "family night." They discovered how the family had become disengaged over time, and had developed not only leisure times together, but also "family work days" when they did yard work together, or cleaned out the garage, or cleaned the house all at the same time. Evelyn took on the responsibility of working out the logistics of coordinating schedules to guard the family time together.

The family counselor is likely to encounter the rationalization, "It's not the quantity but the quality of time you spend with a person that is important." Psychiatrist Armand Nicholi has argued that this statement is designed to rationalize not spending enough time with one's spouse or children: "But as we noted earlier, time is like oxygen. There is a minimal amount that is needed to survive. Less than that amount may cause permanent damage. And I think the same holds true for a child's time and exposure to both parents.

"If we know anything about normal human development, it's that it rests heavily on a close, warm, sustained relationship with both parents."[9] Nicholi has observed that this principle can also be stated negatively: "The lack of time spent between parents and children is a primary cause for the increase in suicide and emotional disorders among children and youth in this country over the past few years.[10]

Family counselors need to inform problem families that healthy family functioning requires large amounts of time committed to one another. Without this time for interaction, it is extremely difficult to resolve family problems.

GOOD FAMILY COMMUNICATION

Strong families have been found to practice good communication. They are good listeners, and they are skilled in expressing their thoughts, desires and emotions to one another. This finding of good communication patterns in strong families is not at all surprising to the family counselor. Even so it is useful for the counselor to point out to families an observation made by Dr. Judson Swihart, an experienced Christian family counselor: " . . . strong families do not automatically have a good communication system. They have to desire it, work at it, reevaluate it and consistently maintain it. Communication requires a constant watchful eye and large doses of nurturing."[11]

It is not unusual for a family to turn to a counselor to help them to resolve problems which have resulted from poor communication practices in family life. Dr. Grace Ketterman illustrated the destructiveness of negative communication by an illustration from her own childhood:

> When I was six years old, I was in first grade in a rural school in central Kansas. One of the exciting times of the year was Christmas time, and it was very much a family time. The school and the church were really the center of family life in our rural community. After Thanksgiving we began preparing for the Christmas program. Every kid in the school, twenty-eight of us and eight grades with only one teacher, would prepare for days on end—making Christmas gifts for our parents, and preparing this wonderful Christmas production of dialogue, carols and poems.
>
> My first year in school I was loving every minute of it. I was so excited about that program. There was only one other first grader—she and I struggled together that first part of the year. She left later on in the school year and I was the only one in my grade for the rest of the year.
>
> But the Christmas program finally arrived. We were all dressed in our very best apparel, although it was not the outstanding quality we are familiar with now. This other little first grader had many more resources than the rest of us, and she was dressed beautifully. She had on a beautiful yellow sweater, a brown pleated skirt and a gorgeous bow tie at the neck of her sweater. I will never forget it. At the end of the little tie were little fuzzie yarn balls.
>
> I was standing on the very front row with little Fran and we were singing "Silent Night, Holy Night." And I reached over and just touched these little balls. I couldn't help myself. I was just so intrigued with them, and they looked so soft. And so here I was singing away, but enjoying those little yarn things.
>
> Well, the evening went along beautifully and it was indeed all I thought it would be. But the next morning at breakfast my mother, a very proper lady, decided that I needed to learn something of the sterner realities of life. She began lecturing me with increasing vigor about how

embarrassed she was the night before: "Didn't you realize that people were laughing? Don't you know that wasn't proper?" And on and on she went.

From the exuberance, joy and excitement of that holiday time, I went into a world that was gray, shallow, empty. A criminal in the dock could not feel much worse than I felt that morning. I recall leaving the breakfast table and crouching in the corner of the kitchen just feeling hopeless, helpless and absolutely worthless.

But a wonderful thing then happened. It's the only time I recall that my mother and father disagreed on any form of discipline or values for us kids. My father came looking for me until he found me. He picked me up so I was on eye level with him and looking me in the eye with his own beautiful brown twinkling eyes said, "Gretchen, I didn't think it was so bad. In fact, it was kind of cute." Hope was restored, my worthwhileness was again within reach—a possibility for me. And my life went on. And indeed Christmas *was* wonderful.[12]

So often in problem families, the family counselor will observe harsh, condemning and critical parents who, although they may have the best of intentions, contribute to a harsh and insensitive communication pattern which is destructive to the family member's well-being.

Because good family communication patterns are hallmarks of adaptive, healthy families, a major goal for family counseling often involves enhancing relationship patterns and teaching families how to communicate with greater skill, effectiveness, and love.

Dr. Ketterman[13] has identified seven characteristics of good communication:

1. Communicators must have minds open and ready to focus on the present issue.

2. Communicators need to keep their intellects equal to or transcendent over their emotions.

3. Communicators will be more successful if they avoid being judgmental or condemning in their attitudes.

4. Communicators will be more successful if they learn

to empathize with each other, but avoid too much sympathy or pity.

5. Communicators do best when they listen with their hearts as well as their heads.

6. Communicators need to keep a clear focus on the goal of each transaction.

7. Communicators need to find a satisfactory balance in the use of assertiveness and gracious deference.

EXPRESSING APPRECIATION

In contrast to problem families, strong families regularly express a great deal of appreciation to one another. They do this by giving sincere compliments, by building each other up psychologically, and by affirming one another. Problem families referred to a family counselor can often benefit by implementing this practice. It is possible to teach family members to express appreciation to one another. When parents model this characteristic, it can be imitated by their children and expressing appreciation encourages similar action from other family members.

Unfortunately, many problem families get caught in a downward cycle of negative criticism sharply delivered to one another. In some families, the members actually look for flaws and faults of others to point out, while ignoring positive features. This destructive input feeds on itself and creates a negative attitude and environment in the family. One of my counseling clients described the absence of appreciation as creating "an emotional desert."

Barbara had an extremely critical attitude toward herself and was often depressed. Her husband, a young pastor, was very encouraging toward her and was a great comfort to her in many ways. In one of the early counseling sessions with the two of them, I asked Barbara to describe her childhood family to me. She explained that her mother was widowed when she was four years of age and never remarried. With great energy, she reared four children in a highly organized household.

Barbara's mother not only imposed perfectionistic demands on the children, but she did it in a highly critical and negative way. No matter how well she did on a report card, her mother chided her, "Why can't you do better?" With chores completed at home, her mother's attitude was, "Yes, but why didn't you see that this needed to be done on your own and just do it without being told?"

As a child, Barbara tried very hard to earn her mother's praise or affirmation. One time she even dared to ask her mother, "Why don't you ever compliment me?"

Her mother sternly replied, "When too many strokes are given, they're not only phony but obviously not deserved. I expect proper conduct, that's your duty, and for that no praise is needed. Besides, it's not my style to dish out flattery."

Eventually, Barbara despaired and gave up trying to please her mother. Even as an adult, she deliberately keeps her visits home as short as possible, and yet her mother's stinging criticisms still devastate her emotionally. She traced her own self-criticism and negative self-concept to her growing-up experience with her mother.

When I asked Barbara what would help in her relationship with her mother, she replied, "I suggested family counseling to my mother a few years ago, but she flatly refused and insisted that she didn't see the need for it. Now what we need is bilateral forgiveness and application of 1 Thessalonians 5:11, Luke 17, James 3 and Ephesians 4:29."

In the meantime, Barbara's husband was helping her to come to grips with her worth and value to God. He often reminded her that she was created in God's own image, that Christ had died for her with an eye to what she could be worth to him, and that now that she had been adopted into God's family, she should view herself as being restored to the image of God.

It takes a great deal of courage for a parent to break through a negative cycle of criticism by expressing honest appreciation for any approximation of cooperativeness in a child. But it is vitally important to take this step. As William James said, "The deepest principle in human nature is the craving to be appreciated."[14]

One of my undergraduate students described this craving to be appreciated in her eleven-year-old brother, Randy. Their family expressed few emotions of any kind. Their father, Alex, prided himself for being "in control" of his emotions and of his family. It was as though the expression of love or tenderness was a sign of weakness.

Randy loved all sorts of sports and excelled in soccer. But his busy parents rarely attended his games. Randy's team got as far as the finals for the state championship, but his dad only stayed for about fifteen minutes of the game before leaving to take care of some personal business. That evening, as Randy excitedly recounted the crucial plays of the game, his father abruptly interrupted, "Of course you did well, what do you expect? Our family down through the generations has always risen to the top. Now settle down and don't get excited. I want you to realize that winning a soccer game is no big deal. Other things in life are more important, like your homework. Go study!"

Randy was crushed. He badly wanted to hear his dad tell him how proud he was. He dashed to the bathroom and locked the door. His older sister was in the hallway and surmised that Randy must have been looking at himself in the mirror when she overheard him softly repeat the words that he had heard other boys' fathers say that afternoon, "Son, I'm proud of you. Son, I'm proud to be the father of such a fine player." Then she overheard Randy crying.

J. Allan Petersen pointed out why expressing appreciation is a quality of strong families.

> Words are creative things and tend to produce what they praise. Words of appreciation draw family members together, create a positive sense of well-being, strengthen the innate self-worth of one another, encourage interdependency, provide a powerful incentive for growth and maturity and unlock the tremendous potential for achievement. All of this, then, has a positive effect on the other qualities of strong families. . . .
>
> Expressed appreciation at home . . . says, "You are important. You are not an orphan. You are on the inside. You belong here. We believe in you. You have great potential."[15]

It becomes an interesting counseling assignment for the family counselor to help a family break through a cycle of negative communication by going around the group and having each one tell why he or she appreciates each other family member. The focus can be first, for example, on the mother. Each child as well as the husband can take a turn expressing why he or she appreciates her in the family. Then another family member can be selected as the recipient of positive feelings, and the family can again go around taking turns expressing appreciation to that second family member. Once all family members have had the opportunity to be the object of appreciation, the family can understand the positive, constructive potential of regularly practicing expressions of appreciation to one another on a daily basis.

A SPIRITUAL COMMITMENT

Many researchers have found that strong families have a high degree of religious orientation and commitment.[16] Dr. Stinnett reported that these families typically state, "God has a purpose for our lives. God is a source of strength for my family and for me as an individual."

"Our awareness of God in our day-to-day life helps us to be less impatient with each other, helps us to get over anger more quickly and helps us to be more supportive and positive in our relationships with each other."[17]

Spiritual values such as love, kindness, tolerance, and support tend to promote positive family relationships. Strong families usually go to church together, have family devotions at home, and encourage one another in their common faith. Researchers found that higher levels of religious involvement are associated with higher levels of satisfaction in marriage.[18] Because a strong spiritual commitment is typically found as a characteristic of strong families, pastors are in a particularly advantageous position to serve as family counselors. Christian family counselors should encourage the positive spiritual growth and development of the families they are counseling as a primary goal.

Responding to Family Needs

Several years ago, the Evangelical Alliance Mission invited me to be the guest speaker for a semiannual field conference in

Vienna, Austria. The missionaries there had discovered that although the people were not rapidly responsive to the gospel, they were more open to share their family problems. In the apartment buildings where they lived, they had many opportunities to meet families, especially those that included children the same ages as their own children. If these missionaries had not had children, they would not have had as many opportunities to minister to the Austrian people. As it happened, most of the children of the missionaries' families in Austria were between five and twelve years of age, so they invited me to lead a ten-day workshop on the developmental needs of families with school-aged children. As a part of this workshop, the missionaries had prepared case studies of families they were helping which we all discussed together. The missionaries met people in their apartment building in the course of everyday living. These people would open up and unload all kinds of marital and parenting problems. Recognizing these needs as potential avenues to building relationships to share the gospel, the missionaries were trying to counsel these families. As we brainstormed counseling approaches for these Austrian families, I think I learned as much or more from them about Austrian family life as they learned from me about counseling methods. We talked and talked for hours about the many challenges of family counseling in that culture and the potential for evangelism in being available to minister to the felt need of their neighbors. By patiently building a helping relationship with these families, the missionaries were eventually able to diagnose a sin problem and present the gospel as the solution.

All family counselors encounter families in which the individual members adhere to a variety of world views and are consumed with a variety of preoccupations. With the intensification of media influences on individuals and the diversity of programing in television, radio, and printed matter, we now have a situation in which no single mentality characterizes all dysfunctional families. Many poor families or families in the Third World may be primarily preoccupied by survival issues or by concerns for justice and political liberation. Middle-class North American families and many European families may be essentially pursuing various preoccupations related to the impoverished values of "personal peace and affluence" as Dr. Francis Schaeffer has labeled them.[19] Different families as well as different individuals in the same family can be caught up with differing problems and preoccupations depending upon their individual beliefs and life circumstances.

In turn, some of the family's life circumstances have been created by the sinful choices made by the family members. Other life circumstances are a general result of the Fall described in Genesis 3. For example, some family members may suffer from the effects of alcoholism or drug abuse brought on by a sequence of deliberate choices by a family member. Children may suffer from the emotional deprivation resulting from a decision by a parent to divorce or from some other tragic circumstance. Victims of family violence suffer from the wrong choices made by the violent perpetrator. Individuals may experience depression and anxiety in response to a family member's chronic practice of sinning against them. Low self-esteem, insecurity, and financial struggles are often by-products of the sinful choices of family members. Because the family is such an intimate environment, the sin of one member can ultimately affect and trouble the relatives of the sinner.

Building a Relationship of Trust

How should the problem of sin be addressed by the family counselor? The Christian family counselor often encounters families in which some members are not "born again" believers.[20] Of course other families counseled are entirely without any converted individuals. Therefore, family counseling becomes an opportunity to share the good news of the gospel of Jesus Christ as the solution to the problem of sin (John 3:16). The challenge is to communicate how the gospel provides an answer to the questions, needs, and preoccupations of the individual unbelievers in the family. Our understanding of Scripture and apologetics can help us to "know how to answer everyone" (Col. 4:6). The Christian counselor should endeavor to provide answers to an individual's own questions regarding a specific point of need.

This task of individually tailoring the Christian answer to a particular person or family often requires that a beneficial and helpful counseling relationship be first established—a fact discovered by the missionaries I met in Vienna, Austria. Apologetics includes a logical factor and an evidential factor, but the delivery of these apologetic factors must typically be accomplished within an effective human relationship. Although the content of the gospel as revealed in Scripture is central to the task of evangelism, the opportunity for presenting that message in a way that will be received by a family depends upon the Christian counselor's relationship with the family.

The very fact that the family has turned to the counselor for help provides a context for their receptivity to the truth of the gospel. Unbelievers' world views are naturally quite tenuous and vulnerable to their own life experience as well as to any penetrating, logical challenge. By maintaining a warm and loving relationship with such a family, the counselor makes it less likely that family members will use such psychological defense mechanisms as denial, rationalization, or intellectualization when confronted with the logical inconsistencies or other inadequacies of their world views.

In this connection the personality, values, attitudes, actions, and beliefs of the family counselor are of critical importance. The family counselor who is attempting to present the gospel can hardly expect the message to be positively received if he or she relates to the unbelieving family members with indifference, depression, agitated conflict, impatience, unkindness, evil intentions, undependability, harshness, or impulsivity.[21] This list of undesirable counselor qualities is the opposite of the list of characteristics presented in Galatians 5:22–23 as the "fruit of the Spirit." It is the work of the Holy Spirit to convict of sin and to lead an individual to repentance, and it is the fruit of the Spirit in the counselor's life which provides the quality of counseling relationship which allows the effective presentation of the gospel to unbelieving family members. This kind of relationship-based approach to evangelism is the approach which is most likely to result in a life-changing conversion in a receptive unbeliever.[22]

The counselor who maintains a relationship which is characterized by empathic understanding, nonpossessive warmth, and genuineness has great potential for effectively accomplishing the task of evangelism. This kind of relationship communicates to the unbelieving family members that the Christian counselor is available to help in the time of their felt need. Of course, the effective family counselor does not merely address the family's spiritual needs for salvation; concrete help is sought and available to address the interpersonal level of conflicts and family dysfunctions. But this very availability of the family counselor to help at the human level of relationship problems promotes receptivity on the part of the unbeliever to accept help for the spiritual needs to relate to God as well.

Presenting the Gospel

Once a strong relationship and rapport have been established with the family, the counselor can take the step recommended by Schaeffer: "The first consideration in our apologetics for modern man . . . is to find the place where his tension exists."[23] That is, the counselor must work with the unbeliever to find the tension between the non-Christian's presuppositions and reality (the reality of the external world or cosmos and the reality of human personality). The next step, according to Schaeffer, is to push the unbeliever toward the logical conclusions of his or her unrealistic presuppositions.

As Schaeffer astutely observed, "every person is somewhere along the line between the real world and the logical conclusion of his or her non-Christian presuppositions. . . . The more logical a man who holds a non-Christian position is to his own presuppositions, the further he is from the real world, and the nearer he is to the real world, the more illogical he is to his presuppositions."[24] Once a relationship is established with an unbelieving family, the Christian counselor should become involved in the demanding intellectual and psychological task of identifying where the unbeliever's point of tension lies, all the while relying on the work of the Holy Spirit.

It is because the unbeliever is "suspended between the real world and the logical conclusions of his presuppositions" that Schaeffer proceeds to the step of moving him "in the natural direction his presuppositions take him."[25] If family members are selfishly pursuing their own "self-fulfillment," the family counselor can point out how this pursuit is logically a self-defeating pattern. Ultimately, the satisfaction and fulfillment that would come from a healthy and stable family relationship will be undermined by excessive selfishness and lack of self-sacrifice—the very behaviors which are supposedly designed to increase one's "self-fulfillment." This is but one illustration of how a family counselor can press for the logical conclusions of an unbeliever's presuppositions about happiness or self-fulfillment.

Schaeffer has observed that every person has built a "roof over his head to shield himself at the point of tension" and that this shelter must next be removed to allow the "truth of the external world, and of what man is, to beat upon him."[26] In the same way the family counselor can help remove some of the rationalizations or other defense mechanisms that family members have erected over their heads to keep the reality of the external world from impinging upon them. This can really help individuals understand their lostness and their state of futility and meaninglessness without a relationship with God. This also helps to pave the way for a presentation of the gospel that makes clear the absolute truthfulness and historicity of the biblical message of salvation and makes clear how the gospel applies to concrete life circumstances.

In the context of an empathic, loving, and genuine relationship, the Christian family counselor is in a good position to ask penetrating questions that effectively "take the roof off" of the unbeliever's illogical and unreal set of presuppositions about life. The trained counselor has skills to minimize psychological defense mechanisms of avoidance, denial, rationalization or the like which keep unbelievers from the truth. But these skills should be used in a positive way, leaving the responsibility of decision to the individuals involved. All coercive approaches such as brainwashing, conditioning, or indoctrination should be avoided.

The main point here is that the family counselor needs to be aware that many of the serious problems that families bring to counseling are due to the reality of sin. In many cases, the magnitude of the destruction of the sin in a family is due to the fact that one or more members of the family do not know Jesus Christ as their personal Lord and Savior. This means that a pivotal task of the family counselor is to effectively communicate the good news of the gospel in a way that will maximize the possibility of receptivity on the part of the unbelievers. In this way ultimate answers can be given to some of the temporal problems being suffered by a family. The very fact that conflicts and struggles are being experienced by a family to such an extent that counseling is sought often provides an opportunity for providing a more realistic view of family relationships and of Scripture's prescriptions for such difficulties. When families who are unbelievers come for counseling, a wonderful opportunity exists to present the power of the gospel of Jesus Christ to heal broken and fragmented relationships. For Christians, the Holy Spirit provides the power and the "fruit" necessary for developing strong and functional family relationships (Galatians 5:22–23).

A family-studies professor at Kansas State University, Dr. Walter Schumm, has convincingly demonstrated how this characteristic of a strong spiritual commitment is the foundation for all the other qualities that make families strong.[27] A spiritual commitment usually underlies commitment to family. And genuine commitment to family is translated in everyday living in terms of the amount of time families spend together. The strong spiritual commitment also motivates (1) the love family members have for one another, (2) spending time together, and (3) expressing appreciation for the family. The combination of those three factors provides the foundation for the development of a good communication pattern. A solid communication pattern combined with spending enough time with each other assures strong families they can then develop strong problem-solving skills—which is the sixth major characteristic of strong families.

PROBLEM SOLVING IN CRISES

Stinnett found that strong families experience crises like any other family but the distinctive feature they have is the reaction of consciously pulling together to cope with problems they encounter. Instead of letting a crisis or source of stress drive family members apart, the strong family deals with bad situations and stressful times in positive, constructive ways. Family members help one another and function as a support system.

Dr. William Wilson, emeritus professor of psychiatry at Duke University Medical School, pointed out that the effective crisis management of strong families has several components:

1. The family has a realistic perception of the crisis event that does not view the crisis as more or less than it truly is.
2. The family maintains an adequate support structure in the community.
3. The family effectively mobilizes resources and makes sacrifices when necessary.
4. The strong family has the ability to anticipate the future and reorganize itself to meet those challenges.
5. The strong family has a philosophy to live by which gives it hope.[28]

Family counselors should point out to problem families that a strong family is not a family that has somehow fortunately been able to avoid any major crises. Instead, strong families experience crises as much as other families but they have developed these components of effective crisis management in order to solve the problems by a joint family effort. This cooperative ability to solve problems in a crisis is perhaps the most complex of the six major qualities of strong families. And yet, much of family counseling takes place when a family experiences a crisis which then precipitates a contact with the family counselor for crisis intervention. Family counselors should realize that merely handling the particular crisis at hand will be inadequate unless the family has been able to learn how to effectively organize itself and function in such a way that it can handle crises successfully in the future.

PROMOTING FAMILY WELLNESS

Families seek family counseling not only because of the presence of relationship problems but because of the absence of the positive qualities that characterize strong families. The research findings reviewed in this chapter have provided a model of healthy, adaptive functioning in a family. By contrast, chapter 2 provided a broad outline of the most common family problems that the counselor would want to look for. The counselor should routinely assess both strengths and weaknesses because counseling a family to become more adaptive requires an identification of their strengths so the family can be encouraged to build on those strengths to overcome their weaknesses. This is a much better strategy than focusing only on problems as much past family counseling did. That was like trying to teach tennis by only pointing out what is going wrong. As Stinnett pointed out, if you want to learn how to play tennis, it doesn't help you to have the coach tell you, "Well, this is how the poor player holds his racket. This is how they approach the ball when it comes to them. This is how poor players stand." What you want a coach to do is tell you how successful tennis players hold the racket, what the successful player does right. So, to help families, the counselor needs a model of healthy, adaptive family functioning to compare to what is present in the family seeking help.

The most constructive approach for the family counselor is to incorporate this research-based model of family wellness in formulating the goals and methods for counseling. As we have emphasized in chapter 3, a negotiation of mutual goals for the counseling process is an important aspect of early stages in family counseling. The family counselor should encourage the family to identify deficits in these areas of family strength and to work toward increasing the qualities which promote family wellness. Hopefully, the family will not be satisfied with the temporary strategy of merely eliminating a particularly stressful family problem but will also have in mind the goal of developing these characteristics of a strong family.

CHAPTER SIX

APPROACHES TO FAMILY COUNSELING

A FAMILY COUNSELOR WILL ENCOUNTER a wide variety of specific problems that are posed by the numerous families requesting help. And yet there are some general overarching goals that these families have in common and there are some general approaches to family counseling that the counselor can use for a wide variety of specific problems. We will see how the counselor can move from a general goal to the initial steps in counseling.

Unlike individual counseling where a counselor is concerned with the well-being of an individual, family counseling is concerned with the welfare of the total family as the members live with one another on a day-to-day basis. One well-used handbook in family therapy[1] suggests that there are five general objectives in counseling families:

1. Promoting normal development and maturation
2. Helping a family function more effectively
3. Reducing discomfort in the family
4. Adjusting to changing situations
5. Helping the family communicate more effectively

PROMOTING NORMAL DEVELOPMENT AND MATURATION

As a general goal, a family should provide an environment that promotes normal growth and development of the family members. The family needs to adjust the way it functions depending upon the age and level of maturity of the family members. Regardless of the specific problem presented to the counselor, the general problem may be that the family is operating in a way that inhibits a child from being able to make normal progress in some area of development. For example, children have a need for more and more independence as they grow older. Yet some families function in a way that does not allow children to mature and do things for themselves. How can a counselor get a family to focus on this problem in ways that would begin to lead to a solution?

Here is an excerpt from an initial counseling session in which the family counselor has used the methods of helping the family identify the problem and helping them understand its causes. Eleven-year-old Aaron was identified by the family as "the problem" because he was displaying regressed behavior for his age. The family included a mother and a father as well as a fifteen-year-old brother and a nine-year-old sister to Aaron. Family members came to the first counseling session evidently prepared with a number of examples of ways that Aaron acted "like a baby." The family counselor has just asked the family members to offer their ideas on why Aaron sometimes behaves in an infantile manner.

Mother: I'll admit that a lot of people have told me that I'm too overprotective of Aaron and I guess I should admit that I imagine that that is part of the trouble here. I don't know why, but maybe I do kind of want to keep him like a baby.

Father: That's really the big cause here. Since he was born, you've always hovered over him and protected him. I don't shield him like that because I want him to be able to learn how to stand on his own two feet and become a man.

Mother: Actually, to tell the truth . . . and I'm sure the counselor here wants us to be honest . . . you really never have been at all caring or affectionate toward Aaron, and I'm not blaming you, because that's just not your personality. To make up for that, I've always had to give Aaron more love, and you call that pampering him.

Counselor: Perhaps you're trying to label who's to blame here for Aaron's problem. You're wondering, is it mother's fault, is it father's fault, or is it Aaron's fault?

Mother: I really don't know. That's why we came here to counseling. I'll admit that at home his dad and I have had a lot of arguments about who's to blame.

Counselor: That implies that you are at least agreeing on one thing—that you don't want Aaron to stay like a baby.

Mother: Why no, of course not. It is really embarrassing when we go out in public, say to a restaurant or something, and Aaron is acting like a baby. I am terribly embarrassed in front of the waitress, and I really don't like him to act that way.

Counselor: I see, on the one hand, you are embarrassed by Aaron's behavior, but on the other hand, there is something inside of you that can't quite bring yourself to give up having him as a baby. So you find it hard to give up this extra mothering. (Counselor turns to Aaron) Can you do without all this attention from your mother?

Aaron: Well, yes . . . I guess I don't really want to give up my mother, I mean, I guess I've kind of gotten used to it.

Mother: But you keep on acting just like a little baby, and I can't stand that.

Counselor: Aaron, let me point out something I've noticed. You're always looking at your mother here in my office and you haven't once looked at your father. Let me ask you something, why don't you look now at your father?

Aaron: Ugh, do I have to look at him?

Counselor: Why would that bother you?

Aaron: Just look at him, doesn't he look mean to you?

(Immediately the brother and sister break out with giggles and laughter.)

Counselor: Oh, so he looks mean to you. Do you mind explaining that?

Aaron: Well, he not only looks mean, but he talks mean with that gruff, loud voice.

Counselor: And so your dad's voice is a lot different from your mom's soft, quiet voice. So you've been looking to your mom for all your needs. You'd rather relate to her, and leave your dad out. But you're missing out on what your dad has to offer you.

Mother: Listen to the counselor, Aaron. He's got a point here. If you avoid your father, you're going to miss out on learning how to be a man. You can't learn that from me, because I'm a female. (Turning from Aaron to the counselor) Now that I think about it, maybe this problem is more involved than I had ever imagined. It's not just keeping Aaron like a baby, but I see what you mean, this is keeping Aaron from learning from his father.

By talking about what he saw going on in the counseling session, the counselor was able to make the family members aware of aspects of the family relationships that were contributing to Aaron's immaturity. Clearly, Aaron needed to become detached from his dependent, infantile relationship with his overprotective mother and develop normal independence in his day-to-day living. But the counselor was also attempting to bring the father and son together. The father needed to reach out to Aaron and Aaron needed to identify with his father in order to progress in his normal development. This family environment had not allowed Aaron to develop a close relationship with his father which could promote male identification. The counselor was actively intervening with questions and interpretations to implement the goal of promoting normal development and maturation.

HELPING A FAMILY FUNCTION MORE EFFECTIVELY

A second broad goal for family counseling is to improve the way in which a family functions in attempting to reach its own objectives. A normal family can set a goal and work together as a group to achieve that goal, but a problem family often gets bogged down. Family members may be confused about what goals should be set, or they may have some goals in mind but not know how to implement them. The counselor needs to clarify family goals and then help the family learn to function in such a way that they can comfortably reach those goals. Here is an excerpt from a counseling session in which the counselor is revealing to a family with two school-age children how much confusion and conflict really does exist in their relationships.

Counselor (deliberately asking a loaded question):   Tell me, who is the boss here in your family?

Mother (Note the significance of the fact that the mother answers first):   Well, I'm not sure. I would have to guess that nobody is.

Father: I would say that maybe both my wife and I are the boss because on some things I have the final say and on other things she does.

Counselor: Let me be a bit more specific. When it comes to the children, who's the boss in discipline?

Father: I'd say that's really her business and not mine. Certainly, she spends a lot more time with them than I do.

Mother: But frankly, that bothers me. I simply don't like to make all these decisions and sometimes I need Frank to just take over and care for the kids.

Father: Well, whenever I tell the kids to do something, you jump in and undermine me, so I don't see why I should even get involved.

Mother: Come on, Frank, you know that's not true. The only time I ever say anything is when you are so angry that you don't make any sense, and that's the only time I interrupt you to protect the kids.

Counselor: You're saying that you only interrupt Frank when he's being unreasonable. Let's see if we can come to some agreement on what is reasonable and what is unreasonable.

Mother: Well, I doubt that we can agree on that.

Counselor: Well, let's just try and see if we can define what is reasonable discipline with the children. Could you describe for me a situation that causes you the most trouble in dealing with the children?

Father: Well, it's just like today. Before we came to this counseling session tonight, the kids came home from school and my wife said she told them they had to do their homework right away. But whenever they don't get it done right after school, then when I get home from work she tells me now it's *my* job to get the kids to do their homework because she's tried already.

Kurt: But I don't want to do more schoolwork right after getting home. I've been working all day at school, so I want to come home and play, especially when it's warm outdoors like this and when it's still light outside. If I did my homework first, it would get too dark to play outside by the time I finished. So I want to play when I first get home.

Beth: Me, too! We're old enough to decide to do our homework whenever we feel like it. After all, it is *our* homework!

Kurt: Yeah, sometimes we don't even have any assignments, but you still yell at us about homework.

Counselor: I see you have a variety of viewpoints about homework. Let's see if you can come to some solution here.

Mother: Well, whenever we've tried to solve this before, we've just ended up getting mad at each other.

Counselor: Okay, I see, the kids prefer to do their homework later in the day, but apparently there are times that they haven't gotten it done. And when you've discussed this, anger has flared. But would you be willing to try to come to some agreement here?

Father: Yes. Let me start by pointing out that it really doesn't matter *when* they do their homework, only *if* they do it at some point in the day. It's their responsibility to get it done.

Mother: But that's the problem. The kids don't do it unless someone supervises them. Who is going to see to it that they get their homework done? You tell me that.

Counselor: Yes, let's talk about that.

Mother: The kids need someone to supervise.

Father: Well, you're the one at home, so I'll let you decide. But don't lean on me if it doesn't get done. That's not something I want to do. Too many cooks spoil the broth.

Mother: That's the problem. He doesn't get involved.

Counselor: Perhaps he doesn't want to be involved and perhaps neither one of you relishes the responsibility for supervising your children in getting their homework done. And as it's worked out, neither one of you has really accepted this responsibility.

Mother: Well, I'll admit to that. In fact, I'm so sick and tired of this whole mess that I wish I could hand the whole thing over to Frank right now—then he'd see how hard it is.

Father: All right. If you want me to do it, I'll show you how to do it right. I'll be in charge of getting the homework done, as long as you promise not to butt in.

Kurt: I'd rather have Dad be in charge.

Beth: Me, too!

The counselor in this session was attempting to improve family functioning by drawing out all the family members to work toward and achieve a common goal. By asking some pointed questions and by guiding the family to stick to the task of problem solving rather than being diverted by expressions of negative emotions, the counselor was able to help the family realize that one of the parents needed to exercise parental authority to insist that the children complete their homework assignments daily.

The counselor offered the interpretation that neither parent wanted to assume this responsibility and that the expectations within the family were unclear at this point. What emerged from the discussion appeared to be a consensus that both children and the mother preferred that the father assume this responsibility and that the father had been attempting to remain uninvolved. The counselor was able to point out the lack of effective parental responsibility in this area in such a way that the previously uninvolved father was challenged to assume the responsibility himself and to clarify that if he accepted the responsibility, he did not want any intrusion from his wife on the matter. By the end of this segment in the session, it appeared that all four family members were agreed on this course of action.

In this case, the precise solution agreed upon by the family members was not as important as the fact that practical problem-solving was encouraged with the involvement of all the family members, that the expectations were clarified, and that some commitment was made for a specific course of action in the future. If the father followed through on his commitment, one would expect future family functioning around the issue of homework assignments to be much improved.

Part of the problem for this family was that they were so caught up in the emotion of the conflict over homework that they had not been able to discern what was going on. They needed to obtain insight into what the problem really was. The counselor brought up the major issue here: Who's the boss in the family? Who's running the show? The family's response was very revealing because the wife, in essence, said that nobody was in charge, but the husband was saying that both he and his wife were in charge. Obviously there was some confusion about family functions.

Starting with this general issue, the counselor then asked the family to get specific about one area of family life, the area of discipline, and then he led them to focus further on an issue that was very current for them, that is, conflict over homework assignments on the very day of the counseling session. The family was able to agree on a number of points. The son and daughter agreed that they didn't want to do their homework right after school. The husband and wife agreed that they preferred not to supervise the homework. The entire family seemed to agree that they had been arguing a lot about the problem.

In spite of this emphasis on agreement, the session ended on a somewhat frustrated and perhaps angry note. The family did not progress to the point of building a better parental coalition. The way that this session ended, Kurt and Beth apparently would not be required to do any homework until their father returned home from work. This arrangement satisfies the children's desire to play after school but may run into a logistic difficulty. If the two parents could cooperate in this situation, a further goal might be for the mother to allow the children to play for a period of time immediately after school, but then require them to start their homework perhaps around an hour before dinner and get some of it done before the father comes home. Then the father could supervise the completion of the homework once he arrives.

Prior to the counseling session, the wife was insisting on one particular arrangement and the husband was insisting on noninvolvement. Therefore, the problem was never solved. When a husband and wife come to an absolute disagreement, Scripture teaches that the husband should be loving toward the wife and not provoke the children to wrath (Ephesians 5:25; 6:4; 1 Peter 3:7; 1 Timothy 3:4) and that the wife should be submissive to the husband. In such a case, the husband could choose to tell the wife, "Okay, we'll do it your way." Or, "The kids can wait until after dinner and do their homework then when I'm at home." If she rigidly held to the idea of having the children complete the homework immediately after having come home from school, she would not be obeying the biblical command to be in submission to her husband.

However, more often than not, if family members are willing to abide by the Christian principle of love, they could work out some agreement together and incorporate the children's desire to have a little free time when they first came home from school. For instance, the children might have fifteen minutes to play when they come home from school and if they had completed their homework the day before, they could extend the time to one hour of play. If they had not, then they would only get fifteen minutes of free time before starting to study. So there are a number of specific agreements that might be negotiated by a counselor in such a situation.

What role should the counselor play in the negotiation process? The counselor would want to provide a model of appropriate problem-solving. He or she would want to help the family discover strategies for coming to a resolution when they come to an impasse on a particular issue. The counselor also becomes a resource person to generate new problem-solving ideas. It is often helpful to say, "Some families try this, other families try this, and still other families have used such and such a solution." The counselor can often generate alternatives for the family to consider and then ask the family members to put together a solution that is comfortable for them. If the family can come together on a solution that everyone agrees to, it is more likely to be implemented. The Christian family counselor also can review some biblical principles of relationship, such as love or the qualities of the fruit of the Spirit, and then ask the family how to apply those principles to their particular situation. This can shift the focus of individual family members from how they can get their own way to how they can be pleasing to God.

REDUCING DISCOMFORT IN THE FAMILY

In general, families that enter family counseling are experiencing considerable discomfort about their situation and a lot of different types of emotions may be involved: frustration, anxiety, anger, sadness, or fears. In general, therefore, the family counselor will attempt to identify these sources of conflict along with their causes. Then, implementing the general goal of decreasing the sources of conflict, the counselor will address the *causes* of the uncomfortable emotions and help the family to gain not only insight into those causes, but also insight into what practical steps to take to reduce their suffering.

Initially, the counselor will try to create a safe counseling environment so that the family members feel free to express and experience these difficult emotions during the counseling session. The element of safety introduced by the "referee" role of the family counselor can often maintain a sense of security and predictability. If several family members start talking at once and try to shout one another down, the counselor can intervene by saying, "Now, wait a minute. Stop. We're only going to have one person at a time talk here." In this way, the counselor can create a structured environment in which the difficult emotions can be dealt with in a helpful way.

I once counseled a family regarding the extreme outbursts of anger of a seven-year-old boy, Chad. Chad had a ten-year-old sister and they lived together with their mother and father. In the home, Chad would not only behave as though he were angry, and state his angry feelings, but he would also hit, pinch, stab, and push his mother and sister when he was angry. These angry outbursts were so numerous each day that the family was in quite a bit of distress.

In dealing with such emotions in a family situation, it is important for the family counselor to recognize that emotions and words that describe emotions do not denote simply a feeling. Emotion words may be used in a way that does not involve a feeling at all, as when someone says, "I *fear* that our economy is in for a recession sometime in the next few years." In the family counseling session, various family members may use an emotion word on occasion not to designate a feeling at all, but merely to express a certain idea. But usually emotion words very much do designate a feeling, and when this is the case, the counselor should remember that such an emotion word never designates only a feeling. Several other elements are implied.

For example, when a person says, "I feel guilt," the guilt is attached to some object,[2] usually some specific wrongdoing. If someone says, "I feel love," that love is attached to some person or some beloved object. If the person says, "I fear," he or she certainly is talking about a feeling, but also that fear has some object—that is, some real or imagined danger.

In the case of the seven-year-old boy in the family I just described, when he said he was angry, there was some object of his anger, that is, some provocation, something that provoked the anger. The counselor, therefore, needs to carefully explore, with a series of questions, what is the object of the emotion that is expressed. In this case, most of the boy's anger was directed at his mother. As we discussed some of the examples of his anger, a pattern emerged.

For example, on one day, this boy, Chad, came to his counseling appointment extremely angry and upset. When I asked why he was angry, his mother explained that she had promised him that he could go to the pet store and buy a turtle. Chad had his heart set on getting the turtle, but when they arrived at the pet store, there was a sign on the window that said, "Closed." Therefore, they went on from the pet store and came on over to their counseling appointment.

I hoped to get Chad to identify the object of that anger by asking him, "Who are you angry at, Chad?"

Chad replied, "I am mad at my mother."

After a series of similar questions, the situation emerged that Chad would typically attach his anger to his mother when the original object of his anger was unavailable to him. The storekeeper for the pet store was gone and had left a sign that the store was temporarily closed. Chad could not express his anger directly at the storekeeper whom he had never met. He then transferred these angry feelings toward his mother, and he was able to see during the family counseling session that his anger toward his mother was unjustified.

Furthermore, exploring his history revealed that he had experienced a series of very painful operations as a young child. He had not been old enough to understand everything that was going on, and he had come to the conclusion that somehow these operations were his mother's fault. So, he was carrying forward from the past a reservoir of hostility and anger toward his mother over the pain he had experienced in his various surgeries.

On that one particular day of counseling, Chad apologized to his mother for having gotten angry at her because he was unable to buy his desired pet turtle. He was able to explain that this was not fair and that he was really angry and frustrated toward the pet store and the shopkeeper who had temporarily closed the store at the very time they went to buy the turtle. He realized that his mother had kept her promise and had taken him to the store and that it was not her fault that the store was temporarily closed.

Furthermore, emotion words logically carry some motivational significance. For example, if you have a fear, that fear not only has an object—what you are afraid of—but that fear also logically conveys a motivation to escape or avoid whatever it is that you are fearing. Similarly, if you are anxious about something, there may also be a motivation to avoid or escape a situation. If you have the emotion of guilt, your motivation would be either to avoid what is making you feel guilty or to make some kind of restitution or to ask for forgiveness. The family counselor can also ask about motivations that are related to emotions, and this helps the family gain more insight into those emotions and learn how to cope with them.

Finally, emotions are such that people have a learned tendency to act on them without deliberate thinking. For example, when Chad felt angry with his mother, he had a tendency to hit her or push her. He didn't stop and think, "Now let me see who is the object of my anger and what I should do to her." Instead, he just automatically lashed out with his aggressive behavior.

The Christian family counselor will not only help a family gain insight into the objects, motivations, and learned tendencies to react automatically to an emotion, but will also remind the family of biblical principles regarding emotions. In the case of the anger expressed by Chad, Ephesians 4:31 and 32 were applicable:

Let all bitterness and wrath and anger and clamor and slander be put away from you along with all malice. And be kind to one another, tender-hearted, forgiving each other, just as God in Christ also has forgiven you (NASB).

In that same passage in an earlier verse (verse 26 NASB) we read, "Be angry, and yet do not sin, do not let the sun go down on your anger, and do not give the devil an opportunity." The family counselor can point out that one should not carry anger over from one day to the next but instead forgive a family member if forgiveness is called for. Verse 25 in this passage says, "Therefore each of you must put off falsehood and speak truthfully to his neighbor, for we are all members of one body." In this case, Chad learned to sort out what was true and what was false with regard to who was responsible for the suffering he had experienced with surgery and who was responsible for the disappointment of not being able to buy his pet turtle at the time he wanted to. He also needed to learn how to forgive his mother and his sister and his father for their actual shortcomings.

ADJUSTING TO CHANGING SITUATIONS

Many different kinds of changing circumstances require a family to make major adjustments. Much of family counseling has the goal of helping families maintain flexibility necessary to accommodate a new experience. For example, a family may move from one city to another. Grandmother may move in with the family to be cared for in her elderly years. A child may move from elementary to middle school with all its after-school activities and clubs. As the family moves from one stage to another stage in the family life cycle, there often has to be a reevaluation of family goals and relationships. Habitual patterns that may have been adaptive when a child was a preschooler no longer work once the child is a teenager.

Often the family counselor will first need to identify the change that has occurred for the family and help the family understand the implications of that change for each family member and for their relationships with one another. For example, if Grandmother has recently moved in with the family and needs to rest during the day because of an illness, it may be that the children can no longer play noisy games in the family room which is adjacent to Grandmother's bedroom. Counselors often focus on rule-making to help a family make the changes it needs to in a flexible way. The counselor would inquire about the rules that were in effect before Grandmother moved into the home. In many cases, the rules have not been stated, they are not entirely clear, or they may be frankly nonexistent. In other cases, rules or expectations that were once effective are now outmoded, forgotten, or no longer enforceable. Sometimes a rule has evolved over time with so many exceptions that it no longer is a useful rule. In our example, perhaps some new rules need to be formulated regarding acceptable behavior during Grandmother's naptime.

In helping the family realize the goal of greater flexibility and adaptation to changes, the counselor often uses a variety of approaches including the following:

1. Helping the family make their rules more explicit and clear.

2. Helping the family consider which rules need to be changed in order to avoid the kinds of conflicts that occur if rules are not clear, seem arbitrary, or are impossible to follow.

3. Helping the family decide how a particular rule might be enforced if a family member violates it. The consequences for rule violations need to be understood by all family members involved.

HELPING THE FAMILY COMMUNICATE EFFECTIVELY

Dolores Curran surveyed people who work with families including pastors, educators, physicians, psychologists, and psychiatrists. She asked them to list the traits of healthy, strong, adaptive families that they knew from their professional work.

A funny thing happened to her research project: She sent out 500 questionnaires and to her amazement 551 completed questionnaires came back to her in the mail. Evidently some people who had received the questionnaire were so enthusiastic about her survey that they made copies of it and gave it to some of their colleagues to complete also. Usually you send out 500 and you hope for maybe a 70 percent return on them. No one expects to get a 110 percent return!

Dr. Curran wrote a book entitled *Traits of a Healthy Family* based on the fifteen traits most commonly reported in strong families by the professionals she surveyed.[3] The first, most commonly reported trait was "the healthy family communicates and listens." That was number one. Number thirteen she paired with that one because number thirteen was "the healthy family fosters table time conversation." Healthy families gather around the table together to talk.

Because good communication in the family is the number one quality found in Curran's research, it is not surprising that helping a family communicate effectively is an important goal in family counseling. Although the family counselor may have negotiated goals with the family, reaching those goals very often depends on the communication patterns going on between family members and the extent to which counseling can improve them. How do family members talk to one another in resolving conflict? How do they listen to one another to promote understanding? In what ways do they communicate to promote growth in individual family members and to mature as a family unit? A central task of family counseling is to help a family develop new communication patterns to resolve conflicts and promote family well-being.

We should remember that before human beings were ever created, there existed perfect love and perfect communication among the members of the Trinity.[4] By contrast, you and I have never seen a family this side of heaven where there has been perfect love and perfect communication. But in those families who have been mature and growing in the faith for a long time, the Lord has had the opportunity to sanctify each member, and they get closer and closer to being true imitators of God in this respect. Ephesians 5:1, 2 NASB admonish us, "Therefore be imitators of God, as beloved children; and walk in love, just as Christ also loved you, and gave Himself up for us . . . ." Counselors can remind Christian families that we are to be imitators of God and that one fact about God is that within the Trinity there is perfect communication.

Counselors, then, often find themselves clarifying meanings for family members, such as the meaning of feelings expressed by a family member. The counselor should also be providing a good model for effective communication. In these ways, the family is helped to give up old habits of incomplete communication, confused communication, and incongruent communication (where verbal behavior and nonverbal communication are saying two different things).

Again, I will illustrate with a case example. Please read this brief excerpt from a counseling session carefully and try to figure out what is wrong with the communication pattern in this family. Ask yourself: What is the counselor trying to do to help the communication process? Is the family communicating in such a way that they are actually missing the real issue that's going on here? If so, what is the family preoccupied with and what is the real issue?

Anna, the mother: I'm confused and tired and frankly, I just don't know what to do, but I'm trying my best to do what I can.

Jeff, the father: Well, perhaps none of us can do any better and sometimes I think we should be realistic enough to admit that no one could do it any better than we do.

Cheryl: Mom and Dad, I know you're both trying.

Jeff: I think, though, we could actually all try even harder. Then maybe . . . (a pause lingers).

Counselor (referring back to something the mother said earlier): A bit ago, Anna implied that she felt like a big failure.

Immediately Cheryl pipes in by insisting: But Mom's not a failure! It just so happens that I don't carry out all her wishes, but that doesn't make her a failure. No way!

Counselor to Cheryl: So you don't want Mom to feel like a failure on account of you, right?

Cheryl: Yeah. She shouldn't think she's a failure, 'cause she's not.

Anna: I certainly feel like a failure, every day. I can't help feeling like I'm the cause of all this mess.

Cheryl (in a disgusted voice): Oh, come off it, Mom, that's baloney. Just stop making those off-the-wall remarks!

Anna: Well, maybe I am off the wall.

Cheryl: This is ridiculous. I just happen to do a few things you don't particularly care for, and then you start talking crazy like that. Can't you just cool it?

Jeff: Now, Cheryl, you know it's only for your own well-being.

Counselor: Could you explain what you mean by that?

Jeff: What her mother tells her is all meant for Cheryl's good.

Counselor: Let's see here. Anna said that she feels like a failure. Anna, do you mean that?

Cheryl: No, she doesn't. She only says that to get me upset. She knows it nauseates me. She knows full well I hate it when she says that. Obviously, she doesn't mean it at all. She's only trying to pin blame on me for something or other— whatever it is.

Counselor: Cheryl, do you feel like your mother is actually shifting the blame to you in this process? You're the failure, is that it?

Cheryl: She makes me feel like I'm causing her to feel like a miserable failure. I'm not saying I'm the real failure or not. I'm not so sure about that. The only thing I'm sure about is that Mom doesn't like anything I do on my own.

Anna: I guess I'm all confused. I'm not sure of anything any more. I thought a mother should do her best for a child and the child should just mind. For instance, I thought it through and decided to tell Cheryl not to associate with Nancy any more but she hasn't obeyed me.

Cheryl: Come off it, Mom. There's nothing wrong with my being friends with Nancy.

Anna: You can see for yourself how rebellious Cheryl really is!

Counselor: So you're saying if Cheryl doesn't obey you all the time, you're automatically a big failure, is that right?

Anna: Well, don't you think you would feel like a failure if you had a teenager who wouldn't obey you?

Counselor: I wonder. Do you want to hear me agree that you are indeed a big failure? Or do you want me to say that you're not any more a failure than I am as a parent? Or do you want me to disagree and insist you're not a failure at all?

Jeff: It seems to me that she's not any more a failure than the typical mother of a teenage daughter. After all, no kid does everything her mother asks her to do.

Anna: Perhaps you're right. All I know is that this whole mess makes me feel terrible inside. Maybe I don't exactly feel like a failure. It's more like the feeling you get when someone doesn't respect you.

Counselor: I see. You would like Cheryl to respect you as a mother. And she can show her respect by obeying you.

Anna: Yes, that's it.

Counselor: And when Cheryl doesn't obey, you respond by feeling rejected as a mother and frustrated. You feel disrespected and somewhat like a failure. What makes you so upset is Cheryl's noncompliance. Actually, you are basically concerned about your problem in controlling Cheryl's behavior.

What's going on in this counseling session? The father seems quite passive. He's just sitting by and letting this conversation go on, without much involvement himself. The mother is anguishing over her inability to get the daughter to obey. She's using an interesting method to gain control. She's coming up with these emotion-laden statements about herself—that she's a failure, that she's confused, that she feels terrible about herself, and that she feels crazy—hoping that these messages will help her regain control over her daughter's behavior. So, one of the problems this family has in communication is that the parents are vague. It's not clear what the precise expectation is for the daughter's behavior, and there is not much unity between the parents. The mother feels that she is out on a limb by herself and from that position she is emoting about feelings.

What's going on with the daughter? Twice the counselor asked the mother a question and the daughter answered. There may be some problems with boundaries in this family—who's the parent and who's in charge here? There are no clear consequences when the mother states a rule and the daughter decides not to comply. The role of the parents is not well-defined. It is the parents' responsibility to clarify what their role is.

In this brief interchange between the daughter and the mother, it seems that the mother's strategy is to try to manipulate the daughter's feelings rather than control her behavior. The mother seems to be preoccupied with the question of assigning blame. She indirectly asks, "Am I to blame when my daughter doesn't do what she's supposed to do?"

The daughter disagrees with her mother, insisting that her mother isn't to blame here. The daughter accurately redefines the situation as a conflict between herself and her mother when she says in effect, "My mother is just saying these things because she knows it bothers me. I want her to cut it out." So Cheryl interprets her mother's comments as criticism of her, which is a correct assessment of what's going on here.[5] By saying, "I'm a failure," the mother is really indirectly criticizing the daughter.

The only input the father has here is his attempt to placate the daughter and the mother by minimizing the problem and not dealing with it: "I don't think my wife's any more a failure than any other mother is. No teenager does everything a parent says anyway."

Of course, the counselor would need to assess the mother's mental stability, but how this mother is feeling about herself may have a lot to do with the nature of her relationship within that family dynamic, including the habitually vague and indirect communication patterns which have developed over time. However, her feelings may also involve some other factors, such as an inadequate view of herself, some long-standing personal problems, distorted thinking, or deep spiritual problems. Accurate diagnosis of her problem is essential. But I am primarily using this little clip from a family counseling session to emphasize how a counselor can help a family work on their communication patterns.

The counselor here knew that emotional feelings are quite subject to redefinition, particularly by somebody in an authority position. There are very few basic physiological states that underlie emotions and yet there are hundreds if not thousands of words we have in our language that denote different shades of emotional feeling. This means that a lot of our interpretation of a particular emotional feeling state has to do with how we are thinking about that experience. If someone, particularly a pastor or a professional counselor, offers us another interpretation, we might buy into it, especially if we're rather vague like this lady who says, "I don't know what's going on. I don't know what my problem is." She might be quite suggestible.

But the counselor should be very cautious in venturing an interpretation, waiting until he or she has seen a definite pattern in a number of statements the person has made over time. The counselor in this counseling excerpt may or may not believe that the mother is a failure, but he told her that he heard her say, in essence, that she's a failure. Obviously, a lot more went on in counseling sessions earlier for him to come up with his interpretations.

The counselor directed the family from their vague and indirect communication patterns to a rather direct and specific interpretation. What the counselor has essentially done so far here is to redefine the mother's earlier statements that she feels like a failure, that she doesn't know what to do as a mother, and that although she's trying, things are not working out. The counselor has helped the mother shift from her feelings of failure to the real issue: her concern over her daughter's conduct.[6] Cheryl is not doing what her mother tells her to do. Now, that move was a step toward clear communication. Of course it will take quite a few more steps to solve the problems here. But notice here, for the moment, how this counselor intervened in a very typical situation where the family communication patterns were muddled.

From a Christian perspective, what biblical principles would you lift up to this family at this point in counseling? This is a key question that the Christian family counselor needs to keep continually in mind throughout all phases of counseling. For Cheryl and her parents, our purpose is not to provide an exhaustive and complete answer, but merely to illustrate some possibilities. The mother's significance should be based on her relationship to God and not on the obedience of her daughter (Psalm 42:5). The husband has some responsibility for affirming and encouraging his wife.[7] Cheryl, the daughter, has an ethical obligation to obey her parents (Ephesians 6:1). The father, furthermore, needs to take the biblical approach to peacemaking. Instead of glossing over the problem and pretending the conflict is not there, he needs to carry out the kind of peacemaking the Bible talks about in the Sermon on the Mount (Matthew 5:9).

The father also has some problems of his own significance, and he has not been taking his biblically mandated role to exercise leadership in his home.[8] He should be a leader rather than being passive. The father here may be overcommitted to work, and in the absence of his direct involvement at home, the children are not receiving consistent discipline. They are therefore living in an insecure environment, and sometimes a daughter like Cheryl is indirectly or even unconsciously recognizing her need for discipline. Ephesians 6:4 teaches, "Fathers, do not exasperate your children; instead, bring them up in the training and instruction of the Lord" (NIV). If this father were really bringing up his daughter in the training and instruction of the Lord, then perhaps she wouldn't be getting so angry and frustrated here. A lot of teaching from the third chapter of James shows the harm of the tongue and that could be some of the spiritual teaching needed by this daughter at this point in time.

Every Christian family counselor needs to have a good grasp of what the Bible says about love and communication between people because one of the main counseling tasks is to clear up communication problems between the family members. Getting a good grasp of Scripture's teaching on anger and the tongue becomes important in Christian counseling of fathers, mothers, and their children. These skills in helping a family communicate have application to counseling nearly all families asking for help.

CHAPTER SEVEN

METHODS OF FAMILY COUNSELING

WHAT ARE SOME OF THE SPECIFIC STRATEGIES and tactics that the counselor can use? That question almost sounds military, as if the counselor were going into a battle. Frankly, sometimes you feel like it after you leave a particularly grueling counseling session. You can feel like you've been on the front lines of a fierce battle. In studying the Bible's teachings on marriage and family relationships in Ephesians 5 and 6, I was struck one time to realize that the context included the end of Ephesians 6, which teaches us to put on the whole armor of God to be adequately prepared for the spiritual battle that we're involved in. It is very interesting to me to consider that family conflicts are often the surface results of underlying spiritual battles. So in considering the major family counseling strategies developed by secular family therapists, the spiritual dimension should not be overlooked and biblical principles should guide and modify the Christian counselor's use of these strategies.

Among the professionals who write about family counseling, there exists considerable disagreement about which methods are most effective for producing helpful changes in family functioning. Part of this disagreement is a result of the lack of any generally agreed upon core of family theory[1] and a result of a diversity of preferences among a number of theories or models of family counseling (see Appendix 1). Furthermore, although an increasing number of researchers have been studying the effectiveness of family counseling,[2] the publications tend to report the use of a global approach, such as "strategic," "structural," "communicational" or "conjoint family therapy," instead of systematically investigating the effectiveness of specific intervention strategies.[3] Furthermore, many family counseling models share the use of many specific intervention strategies which they have in common,[4] and, in practice, most family counselors are "eclectic"[5] and therefore use a variety of strategies derived from the different models. For these reasons, this chapter on family counseling methods will be practical and focus on the commonly used intervention strategies themselves.

Experienced family counselors from a variety of theoretical orientations have found that a number of intervention strategies are particularly helpful during the earlier stages of family counseling. The chart on the next page lists five of these strategies together with a description of each.

Although these strategies are particularly useful early in counseling a family, the skilled family counselor will use any of these interventions throughout the counseling process where appropriate.

DIRECT INTERVENTION

In early family sessions, the counselor will observe a pattern of family interaction that obviously needs to be changed. The pattern of interaction is not biblical. It's not healthy. It's destructive. Not wanting to let that interchange go by without comment, the counselor may need to directly intervene just at the time the negative interactions occur in the counseling session.[7] The counselor confronts the family quickly and precisely at the point when he or she notices a destructive pattern taking place. A counselor who is too passive or too permissive may turn out to be quite ineffective. Such direct intervention is often necessary in order to spark the family into their own actions. The family may be trapped in a cycle of interaction patterns that have become a habit over time. By observing a destructive interaction pattern and immediately intervening, the counselor can assist the family to overcome barriers to changes.

Probing for Feelings

There are a variety of ways to intervene directly with a family. One tactic is to probe for feelings that are being suppressed and not being overtly stated. In the case of Cheryl and her parents in the last chapter, the counselor probed for the mother's feeling of being a failure. Up until that point in counseling, the mother hadn't expressed those feelings in so many words, but the counselor was probing to see how she was feeling and to bring out into the open some submerged perceptions. In this way, the counselor moves into the deeper meanings of family interaction, instead of letting the family operate on a superficial level. Cheryl's family was focusing on the question of who was to blame, but that was a superficial understanding of what was really going on. The deeper issue was the daughter's disobedient behavior. The counselor actively intervened to get down to that deeper meaning which was underlying the surface conflict. The counselor moved beyond the presenting problem the family gave him, and he identified the real underlying issue. The counselor can use questioning to probe for feelings and to move into deeper meanings. Perceptive questions are often more effective than overstatement or direct interpretation.

Strategies Commonly Used in Early Stages
of Family Counseling[6]

1. Joining

   The counselor establishes a working alliance with the family system as a whole and with all the individual family members. This is done by initially accepting the way the family is organized and its style of interacting, and by showing a willingness to adapt to the family's style instead of imposing one's own style.

2. Probing

   The counselor makes certain comments or gives certain directions during the family session for the purpose of trying to understand the family's strengths, structure, potential flexibility, and possible areas of change. In the process, the counselor may bring to light a number of aspects of the family's structure which have been underground or not apparent to family members.

3. Drawing Out Stress or Conflict

   After identifying a family pattern of avoiding or ineffectively dealing with stress or conflict, the counselor helps the family change by (1) directly facing stress or bringing a confrontation out in the open, (2) drawing attention to differences in opinions or behaviors that the family usually minimizes or ignores, (3) not allowing problematic communication patterns (such as blocking the family member who interrupts others who are talking), or (4) siding with one family member or one subsystem against another in a family conflict.

4. Defusing Unproductive Conflict

   The counselor directly stops the family engaged in a runaway argument or escalated conflict which is a "re-run" of a script which does not end in constructive problem-solving, which consists primarily of negativism outcomes and lack of mutual supportiveness, and which results in increased suspicion and mistrust.

146

5. Encouraging Individual Boundaries	The counselor has the family members practice treating one another as individuals to be respected, by (1) asking family members to speak directly to one another rather than talking about one another, (2) not allowing other family members to answer questions or speak for the individual spoken to by someone else, (3) helping the family develop rules for carefully listening to what others in the family say, (4) emphasizing that the family needs to allow differences in what is considered appropriate among the children of different ages, (5) encouraging the courtesy of allowing only one person to be talking at a time without inappropriate interruption by other conversation, and (6) discouraging the family member from acting as the spokesperson or memory bank for the family.

Uncovering Destructive Patterns

The family counselor can directly intervene in a number of other ways. He or she can guide a family into deeper interaction by pointing out a process such as scapegoating.[8] In other instances, the counselor will lead the family to face a difficult issue instead of letting them digress on a tangent or skirt the painful subject. In still other cases, the counselor will note that a statement has more than one meaning, as in a "joke" which is thinly veiling hostility.

A counselor observed during a counseling session that whenever the father would turn to his fourteen-year-old son, Mike, he would become noticeably louder and raise his voice at him.[9] The counselor interpreted this reaction as the father's annoyance toward Mike, but during the family session Mike said that he could not see that he was doing anything that would cause his dad to get angry. The father was not specifically telling Mike what he was doing wrong. The father was just giving a message of irritation at the son by means of his change in voice inflection.

The counselor continued to observe this in the sessions and discovered a pattern: The father would talk to Mike in this irritated voice right after his wife had been critical of his competence as a father. The wife complained about her husband's inability to discipline Mike properly. So when the mother criticized the father, the father became irritated and directed his hostility toward the son. In the meantime, Mike wasn't getting a clear message as to what he should or should not be doing, and he was getting quite angry at what he perceived to be an injustice toward him.

The counselor could see that the father was actually provoking the son and gently pointed out that he might be violating the Ephesians 6:4 passage, "Fathers, do not exasperate your children . . . ." Then the counselor used a rather direct question of the father to directly intervene in this case: "What is really making you frustrated and angry?" In this way, the counselor interpreted the meaning behind the father's hostility. He had an unresolved relationship problem with his wife, but he was turning his frustration on to his son. To lighten the pain of this insight, the counselor described that old cartoon where the boss yells at the father. He comes home and yells at his wife. The wife yells at the kid, and the kid goes out and kicks the family dog. This illustrated the common problem of displaced hostility.

Applying Biblical Counseling Principles

Advising. With this family, this Christian counselor applied several biblical principles. We find the word "counsel" in several places in Scripture where it describes a process of imparting wisdom or knowledge (e.g., Exodus 18:19; Judges 20:7, 18, 23; Proverbs 12:15; 19:20; and Jeremiah 38:15). Acts 5:33, Acts 27:39, and Luke 14:31 use the word "counsel" to mean "to consult." In Revelation 3:18 "counsel" means "advise, give authoritative instructions." Often the Christian counselor in such a situation must give some direct consultation or advice. When the counselor observes a destructive pattern going on in a family, the counselor needs to point it out in a way that family can understand. This can fulfill the biblical concept of giving counsel.

Comforting. The word "comfort" is also used in Scripture to refer to a helping relationship. In this counseling situation, Mike needed some comfort in his situation of suffering unjustly. The importance of comforting a troubled person is taught in Luke 6:24; Acts 9:31; Romans 8:24–28; and 1 Corinthians 14:3. Sometimes "comfort" is used in the sense of consolation or encouragement (2 Thessalonians 2:16). And "comfort" in Colossians 4:11 denotes soothing or solace. Fourteen-year-old Mike was getting angry because of the displaced hostility dumped on him by his father. The counselor therefore used empathy and reassurance to comfort the boy during the counseling session.

Exhorting. But first, the counselor exhorted this father to apologize to his son for unfairly dumping negative emotions on him. "To exhort" means "to urge or entreat to proper action." We find this word used in Philippians 4:2; 1 Thessalonians 4:10 and 5:14; Hebrews 13:19–22; 1 Timothy 1:3 and 5:1; and 2 Corinthians 8:6 and 12:18. Exhortation has a future perspective; it calls for action. Fortunately, the father saw the problem once it was pointed out to him, and he felt genuine remorse for provoking his son. It took time for the son to respond positively to his dad's apology, and the counselor exhorted him to forgive his father as Christ had forgiven him. Eventually, Mike chose to follow this wise counsel.

Teaching. The counselor needed to actively teach these family members some truths from Scripture. In Scripture, the word "teach" is sometimes used in the absolute sense of giving instruction (such as in Matthew 4:23 and 9:35; Romans 12:7; 1 Corinthians 4:17). In other cases (such as in Matthew 5:2 and Matthew 7:29), it is used in the sense of teaching the truth. Counselors may need to teach family members some things about biblical principles and about communication, forgiveness, and love. Active intervention includes all these strategies and involves these different biblical components.

Interventions Focusing on Husbands

Research conducted at a family counseling center at a midwestern university found that five family counseling strategies were associated with husbands and fathers feeling better about themselves in general after counseling had ended. This chart lists and defines these five strategies:

Counseling Strategies Associated with Husbands' Positive Evaluations of Their Lives and Marriages[10]

1. **Providing Advice** — The counselor describes how family research findings apply to the situation, provides information on the normal needs of children at various stages of development, and recommends articles or books for family members to read.

2. **Allowing Expression of Typical Family Transactions** — The counselor deliberately takes a peripheral observer role for part of the session to permit the family system or a family subsystem to reveal its usual pattern of interaction.

3. **Replacing Inappropriate Boundaries** — The counselor induces changes in the problem-causing inappropriate boundaries between family members, such as by taking a child out of a parentlike role, by extracting a child from being used by parents to express their marital conflicts (triangulation), or by dismantling chronic cross-generational coalitions (such as child and parent vs. parent, or extended family member and one parent vs. other parent).

4. **Encouraging Appropriate Boundaries** — The counselor helps the family to establish firmer boundaries between the subsystems that are differentiated by family generations, that is, he or she encourages the boundaries that distinguish the sibling subsystem, the extended family group, and nonfamily groups.

5. Giving a Paradoxical Recommendation	The counselor induces a change in the family's rules of interacting by delivering a recommendation that is carefully phased (1) to advise the family or a family member to keep doing something they expect to be changed by counseling, (2) to imply that this advice will lead to change, and (3) to thereby create a paradoxical tension because the family is instructed to change by continuing to be the same.*

*The Christian counselor will want to carefully analyze the ethical implications of endorsing an existing family interaction to avoid being understood as recommending a sinful pattern. Therefore, this intervention strategy is rarely, if ever, appropriate for a Christian counselor.

The husband/fathers in troubled families are often peripheral, underinvolved family members. It makes sense, therefore, that the counseling strategies which contributed to their satisfaction were active boundary-marking interventions that often directed these men toward becoming more engaged in both the marital and parental subsystems of their families. Research has indicated that it is important for the family counselor to get the disengaged family member actively involved early in the counseling sessions. The family counselor who is successful may very well be the one who is able to quickly form a therapeutic alliance with family members, diagnose problems in family structure, affirm strengths in the family, and then move rapidly and actively to alter family structure with these boundary-marking interventions.[11]

Interventions Focusing on Wives

The family counseling strategies which were found to be associated with positive evaluations of the wives' own marriages and lives in general after counseling are presented in this chart:

Counseling Strategies Associated with Wives' Positive Evaluations of Their Lives and Marriages[12]

1. Tracking and Affirming	Instead of initiating an action, the counselor follows the family's own communication and behavior patterns in a way that (1) encourages them to continue providing information, (2) affirms individuals or the family as a whole, and (3) provides the backdrop for later active change-producing strategies.
2. Redefining Who Owns the Problem	The counselor either (1) broadens the family's understanding of an individual's problem to include the related family interaction patterns, or (2) momentarily refocuses the family's attention to a family problem from the symptom of one family member to the symptom in another member.
3. Reframing	The counselor redescribes a behavior, a symptom or an attitude in a different framework that appears more positive and socially acceptable. Although the counselor does not directly encourage the family or an individual in the family to change that behavior, the way they think about that behavior changes in a way that leads to different family interactions and consequently to new behavior patterns in the family.
4. Allowing Expression of Typical Family	The counselor deliberately takes a peripheral observer role for part of the session to permit the family system or a family subsystem to reveal its usual pattern of interaction.

Unlike the intervention strategies associated with the husbands' ratings of satisfaction after counseling, this list for the wives showed that their favorable responses were associated with a set of somewhat gentle tactics which did not actively challenge the family's structure. Frequently, the wife is relatively overinvolved in the family and is exerting a great deal of emotional energy to maintain her central position. Challenging her pivotal role in keeping the family together would often be a mistake because the positive contribution of her role cannot be overlooked.[13] Instead, it may be more useful to recognize, identify and accept her positive role, and then reframe the presenting problem for the wife/mother who is perhaps the most highly involved and frustrated family member with regard to that problem.

REMEDIAL GUIDANCE

Another set of counseling strategies is even more active than "direct intervention." "Remedial guidance" is needed in some highly disorganized families that have disintegrated to such a point that they are in tremendous disarray. Because of the floundering confusion of these marginal family units, aggressive guidance is necessary to lead them to some relief. Such families are suffering so much chaos and pain that they are unable to set realistic goals and make any progress toward them.

The counselor uses a very basic, remedial level of direct guidance to lead family members to set goals, follow his or her directions for achieving them, and thereby shift from a disorganized state to a program of positive change. When there's an absence of a biblical leadership pattern in the family, the counselor may have to model the kind of leadership that he or she then hopes that the father or single-parent mother will emulate. With tremendous disorganization, there's also a lot of confusion. To get things moving, the counselor may have to intervene even more strongly than normally desired. The counselor assumes a lot of leadership at first to guide and steer the way through the confusion and disorganization. Remedial guidance is much like the extreme you would have to take to get through a jungle where there's no road. You would have to get some tractors and earth movers to push through a dirt road heading out of the jungle.

Biblical Sternness

In this case, the biblical terms "admonish" and "rebuke" often might be involved. "Admonish" is a good counseling word for disorganized families (Romans 15:14; 1 Corinthians

4:14; Ephesians 6:4; Colossians 1:28 and 3:16; 1 Thessalonians 5:12–14; and 2 Thessalonians 3:15). Admonition involves instruction, but it also includes a warning about dangers, particularly in a corrective sense to those for whom danger is imminent because of disobedience. It involves warning people to stop living in ways that are leading them away from God, and instructing them to adhere to biblical injunctions. The counselor may see that a disorganized alcoholic or drug-abusing family really needs admonishment, especially those families with some church background and Christian training. They need to be brought face-to-face with God's commands in Scripture.

"Rebuke" is another word used in the Bible for counseling. It refers to pointing out or convincing people of their fault or error. This word occurs frequently in the Old Testament in Psalms and Proverbs in the sense of corrective instruction. In 2 Timothy 4:2, "rebuke" has the force of a command. Jesus rebuked the disciples (Mark 8:33, Luke 9:55). Similarly, a counselor can build up the family by rebuking them for identifiable sins that have contributed to their chaotic ways. With remedial guidance for the family which is disorganized and confused, the counselor helps the family develop sensible rules based in biblical principles, helps the family members to follow those rules, and helps the family to develop a sense of unity and of working toward a common purpose as a way to pull out of their confused state.

Humility

Family counselors who intervene and directly guide families should do so with a certain amount of humility, recognizing their limited knowledge about the complexities involved for a given family. Before a family comes in for a session, it is especially important for the Christian counselor to pray that the Holy Spirit will give insight into the dynamics underlying the family's real problems. The counselor can pray, "Help me to understand in my own mind what is going on."

Only God is omniscient. He knows the whole story. The counselor is given only part of the data by the family. Therefore, the counselor should pray that God would guide the session in such a way as to have the relevant details surface. A counselor can ask God to prompt him or her to ask the right questions that will lead to revealing what the real situation is (Hebrews 4:16; 1 Thessalonians 5:17; James 4:2; John 16:24; Philippians 4:19; Luke 21:36).

The longer you counsel people, the more you can see regularities in family problems. Apparently there are only a finite number of ways that people can sin against each other and not only do you eventually see the same problems from family to family, but you also observe how an individual family itself tends to repeat the same kinds of mistakes over and over. People do have some degree of creativity, but I don't think God has given us a very great facility to be uniquely creative in how to sin.

Even counselors who have accumulated a lot of experience may encounter a family which really stumps them. Occasionally, the counselor just can't figure out what's going on. I knew one very experienced Christian psychologist in Southern California who had been counseling for about thirty years. He described a challenging case to me one time and said that, frankly, he was "just fishing." He couldn't figure out what in the world was going on, but he had prayed that he would be able to sort out the problem. Then in the second session, he asked just the right question that brought out the whole family dynamic. He said he did not believe that happened accidentally, but that God was guiding him in what to ask. As far as he was concerned in his own mind, he was "just fishing" at random—just letting the line out any place on the lake without knowing exactly where the fish were.

Any counselor, whether experienced or not, will find that there are some cases that need to be referred to a different counselor. It is wise for a counselor to recognize when he or she is not the most helpful person for a given family. No matter what a particular counselor's training, experience, or capabilities, there are cases when someone else would be more effective.

If you are counseling a family with few results and are continually thinking, "What's going on here?" it is very wise to consult with someone else. Describe the situation and see if they can help you gain insight into that family's problems. If that doesn't help sufficiently, then consider referring the family to someone else. In some cases, you cannot make much headway simply because of the interaction of your personality and family members' personalities. The interaction of personalities may not be optimal. I think we should all be humble enough to recognize that when it happens.

A Christian counselor I know in the Midwest does primarily marriage counseling. He told me one time that after the first three years in operating a new Christian marriage counseling center he had a 100 percent success rate. I asked him what he meant, and he replied with enthusiasm, "Not one couple has filed for divorce."

I rejoiced with him regarding that statistic on preserved marriages, but I thought to myself that successful marriage counseling should result in more than just preventing a legal divorce. Not all couples who come for marriage counseling are considering divorce. Their concern may be focused on something entirely different. I wondered if this Minnesota counselor had accurately diagnosed the problems of those couples. Somehow he was claiming a better success rate than Jesus had.

A Christian counselor must recognize that he or she does not have the power to solve all the family's problems. Only God is ultimately sovereign. You may have a very accurate diagnosis and a very good technique, but some families choose not to improve no matter what you do. Jesus experienced this same kind of rejection of his wise counsel (see Luke 18:18–23).

INTERPRETATION STATEMENTS

Interpretations are direct statements to the counselee, such as, "You are sad about this." "You feel betrayed." "You felt rejected and this hurts you deeply." "You feel that no one in the family understands you."[14] Such statements may call attention to feelings, motivations, states of mind, or spiritual condition. The Christian counselor may offer interpretations of the person's relationship to God, "You're feeling very distant to God." Or, "As you consider your behavior in light of God's moral law, you're feeling very guilty." Sometimes a counselor interprets silence during the session. A family talks back and forth in a session and one family member is asked a question by another family member but doesn't respond. The counselor may say, "You'd rather not talk about that today. Do you know why you are sensitive about this issue?"

On other occasions, the counselor might interpret behavior to the family. For example, during a counseling session, a thirteen-year-old daughter precipitates a heated debate between her father and mother by cleverly uttering certain pronouncements that she knows her parents will respond to with opposite stances. She knows from past history in the family that there is a certain topic on which her parents take opposite sides. So she gets her parents going with an argument by simply bringing up that issue. The perceptive counselor then may interpret that interaction in the family by pointing out that the daughter has, in effect, provoked an argument by deliberately bringing up a controversial issue between the parents.[15] In this way, she has successfully removed attention from herself, to deflect a conversation regarding her own responsibility for her problem.

The counseling tactic here is to interpret how the family is operating in such a situation by referring to individual behavior and to family system dynamics. Family members can be so close to the situation—so caught up in that behavior pattern—that they may not see it themselves. The counselor enjoys the great advantage of being an outsider.

The counselor may have seen the daughter do this several times and now the realization dawns: "Well, this is a pattern. Whenever the father starts talking about the daughter's responsibility, she brings up issue A, B, or C where the parents disagree. Then this gets the parents engaged in an old argument, successfully deflecting the conversation from the daughter's behavior." Such interpretations come from experience in working with people and in working with families.

The counselor can be dead right on an interpretation, and some family members will readily acknowledge it, while others will flatly deny it by insisting, "No, that's *not* going on." Denial, as you may know, is a psychological defense mechanism, and often the closer a counselor gets to the truth, the louder a counselee will yell, "No, that's not happening." That doesn't mean the counselor's interpretation is wrong.

To get around the defense mechanism of denial, you might offer an interpretation in a tentative way. You might say, "It appears to me that what may be happening here when Tammy brings up this controversial issue is this . . ." Another way to make an interpretation tentative is to suggest that it may be an "unconscious" process, which indeed may be the case. Tammy doesn't fully realize what she's doing, but she unconsciously learned this habit of getting out of the limelight by bringing up a controversial issue. The counselor may say, "Tammy may or may not realize that what she's doing is deflecting attention from her own responsibility by bringing up this issue that she knows mom and dad disagree on. Do any of you see this happening? As you think about it, could that possibly be what's going on here?"

Offering the interpretation hedged about with tentative words like "may be," "possible," "could it be" makes it less threatening to the family, and they can stop and think about it without responding with the psychological "reflex" of denial or another defensive maneuver. If the counselor makes an interpretation of the family very boldly, as though speaking an infallible, inerrant word, then it's much easier for the family members to deny it.

CHECKING THE FACTS

For a number of years, I taught an undergraduate university course entitled "Family Relationships." Each semester, I invited a number of clergy from different denominations and faiths to participate in a class panel to respond to students' questions on such issues as interfaith marriages, premarriage counseling requirements in their churches, sexual ethics, and church teachings on marriage and parent-child relationships.

One semester when I called one of the Protestant pastors (whom the students particularly liked) to invite him to that semester's panel, he accepted and then asked if I would accept a referral of a family he had been counseling. "I'm really stuck with this family. They are regular members of my church and they participate enthusiastically, but when they come in for family counseling, they all get so emotional and upset with each other that they just argue and fight in front of me. I'm having a tough time making any progress. Maybe it's because alcoholism is involved, and I don't know much about how that affects a person and their family. In any event, I'm so pressed for time right now that I don't have the time to read up on alcoholism, so do you have any openings to see them at your office?" Although my schedule was tight at the time, I agreed to fit them in because this pastor had been so gracious to participate in my course from semester to semester.

Pete and Laura came in the next day with their fifteen-year-old daughter, Melodie, who was the mother's biological daughter by a previous marriage to a drug addict who abandoned them. Laura had married Pete eleven years ago, but they had been separated three times for varying lengths of time. Laura was a chronic alcoholic. She had had a problem with alcohol for over eighteen years. Three years ago, she and Pete became close friends with some neighbors who took them to their church. They attended for about three months before Laura and Pete had a major argument, after which Pete left Laura and Melodie and moved out of state to where his parents lived. While out of state, Pete attended another church's revival services where he decided to confess his sins, accept Jesus Christ as his personal Savior, and live his life to please God instead of himself. He immediately realized that he should return to his wife and provide support for his family. He had returned to his wife only three months before I agreed with his pastor to see the family for counseling.

Pete was only partially employed, looking for full-time work in construction, and this was a stress on him and the family. But he expressed the attitude, "I want to be a better father and husband than I have ever been. I've never really been responsible to my family." Before becoming a Christian, Pete had abused a number of illegal drugs, on and off, and he still struggled with yielding to that temptation. He also had a tense and critical personality, and would unpredictably erupt into extreme anger, hostility, and rage at the slightest provocation.

Laura had only recently become more involved in church, at Pete's insistence, after Pete had returned home and convinced her that the Christian faith was the key to restoring their marriage. She was still growing in her awareness of her spiritual needs, but she was open to the Christian faith, and she appreciated the supportiveness of the church members who had befriended her.

In the meantime, fifteen-year-old Melodie was having chronic school problems and had developed the pattern for two years of largely ignoring her mother's requests. Pete was trying to help Laura gain some parental control over Melodie's behavior. They had explained a number of new family rules to Melodie recently, and the central crisis issue this family brought to me at the first counseling session was Melodie's failure to come home after school the day before. She had stayed overnight with a friend and returned to school the next morning. Laura had called the school that morning and learned that she was in class, and Pete arrived at Melodie's last class for the day to pick her up to come to the family counseling session.

This first session began with Laura's description of Melodie's pattern of disobedient behavior and temper tantrums at home. Pete essentially confirmed the difficulty, admitting that he had only compounded the problem by leaving the family and failing to provide them any support. But he insisted that he was rededicated to being a faithful father and husband.

Then Melodie attacked Pete for "humiliating her" by showing up at school to pick her up, and she pointedly told him that if he really wanted to be a better father he should give her more freedom and stop interfering with her plans.

Laura angrily retorted by arguing that Melodie had created her own dilemma by failing to come home the night before, so there was no way she could have told her about the counseling appointment in advance.

Melodie insulted her mother by telling me, "She's the one that needs a shrink. She staggers around the house all day with a bottle of beer in her hand."

Pete interrupted to demand that Melodie show more respect for her mother, to which Melodie retorted, "Pete, you're some example! You've never been much of a dad, and besides, what do you know about respect after all the times you've slapped and shoved Mom around."

With his face flushed red with anger, Pete counterattacked by telling Melodie, "You should talk, Melodie, you've hit your mother more times than I have."

Laura sternly raised her voice to Melodie, "Tell the truth for once, Melodie, you just hit me Monday after I walked into your room only to find you and Benny sleeping together. You've never been anything but a slut and a whore, and the next thing I expect to find out is that you're pregnant."

Within the first five or so minutes of this family counseling session, a number of serious conflicts and problems had emerged. Pete, Laura, and Melodie were all highly involved with these conflicts, and serious allegations were flying. The family counselor needs to realize that in such a heated situation each family member might have the tendency to exaggerate or distort the facts of the situation to suit their argument.

Melodie might have been surprised, disappointed and a bit embarrassed to have her stepfather show up at the classroom door at the end of class to pick her up, but she was exaggerating when she said she was "humiliated." Although Laura admittedly had a problem with alcohol, it was an exaggeration for Melodie to say she "staggered all day with a bottle." In the heat of an argument, it was not clear how much the daughter and the husband had physically abused Laura. And Laura's accusation that Melodie had "never been anything but" sexually promiscuous was also an exaggerated statement in the course of intense ventilation of emotions.

Counselors can become frustrated and baffled by family sessions like this which are characterized by such highly explosive feelings. But the counselor can be an effective helper by remaining calm and objective. Before the family will be able to solve its problems, it will need to assess its problems more accurately and reasonably. The counseling tactic of "checking the facts" can be of help at this point.

The counselor might say, "Now, let's back up and take just one thing at a time. Melodie, the fact that Pete picked you up at school this afternoon seems to imply that you didn't tell your mother and father that you were planning to stay overnight at a friend's house. Is that true?"

Melodie: Yeah.

Counselor: Did you know that your parents had made it a rule recently that you are supposed to let them know where you are after school?

By raising questions that "check the facts," the counselor helps family members assume direct responsibility for their own behavior.[16] It also heads off the strategy of someone like Melodie who uses counterattacks upon other family members as a way to avoid facing her own personal responsibility.

The tactic of "checking the facts" is not limited to dates, times, specific behaviors, and circumstances, although it will often be useful to focus on these matters. The "facts" include emotional and moral matters as well. For example, with the family of Pete, Laura and Melodie, a relevant fact would be the matter of broken trust. Now that Melodie has stayed overnight at a friend's house, what has happened to the parent-daughter trust level? What happened to the trust level when Laura discovered Benny in Melodie's bed? The counselor can focus attention on Laura's lost trust in Melodie, stressing that it will take a long period of time to rebuild a trusting relationship again. It takes a long time of good, predictable behavior to earn trust back again. So "checking the facts" involves asking specific questions that help family members focus on behaviors, events, thoughts, emotions, ethics, and situations in a way that avoids exaggeration or distortion.

BEHAVIOR CHANGE TACTICS

The problems suffered by the family of Pete, Laura, and Melodie required specific behavior change tactics, as is the case for many troubled families. It would take an entire book to tell how this particular family improved, and such a book might very well provide the plot for an exciting "made-for-TV" movie. Unfortunately, space does not permit me to finish the drama of this family's story here. Instead, I've adapted a summary chart from the *Journal of Marital and Family Therapy* to define the basic family counseling strategies for changing behavior patterns in such a family:

Strategies for Changing Specific Behavior Patterns[17]

1. Modeling	The counselor demonstrates a behavior or way of communicating that he/she has recommended that family members try. Examples of modeling include (1) using a new way to nurture or discipline a child, (2) talking to children in ways that take into account their ages and developmental levels, (3) directly confronting an issue, (4) revealing one's thoughts, beliefs, or emotions, and (5) demonstrating parental control.
2. Prescribing In-Session Behavior	During the counseling session, the counselor directs family members as to where they should sit, who they should talk to, and when they should interact in other ways.
3. Child Behavior Management	The counselor trains the parents how to record baseline data on problem child behaviors in the home, and provides instruction and supervision on how to set clear expectations for appropriate behavior and use reinforcement procedures to influence child behavior.
4. Mutual Contracting	The counselor negotiates an agreement whereby the husband and wife each consent to simultaneously change some aspect of their behavior, according to their spouse's desire as an exchange or "trade-off."
5. Good Faith Contract	The counselor conducts parallel negotiations with a husband and wife in which the husband agrees to a change in his behavior with a contracted reward for successful instances, and the wife agrees to a separate change in her behavior with a contracted reward for successful instances, and these two contracts are not dependent upon one another in terms of being carried out on a daily basis.

DIRECTING CHANGES

The counselor may have appropriate opportunities to direct changes in family relationships. For a particular family, you may have the goal that relationships should be more cooperative, that the family members need to collaborate with one another in solving problems. But occasionally, family members are unaware of some aspect of competition in their relationships. They may not be aware of what is causing a stalemate and so the counselor may need to change some relationships by teaching new ways of working with one another to solve problems.

Several strategies have been developed by family therapists for establishing new relationship skills in families. The chart on page 165 outlines three of these methods.

Changing Alignments

In other cases, the counselor may direct changes in alignments in a family. Often the first step is to bring faulty alignments to the attention of the family. Family members may not be completely aware of the dynamics underlying their relationships, and the counselor, as an outside observer, can help them understand what is going on.

For example, Gregory and Jane sought counseling because they and their two children argued constantly. Over several sessions, the counselor observed that Jane's very strong alignment with thirteen-year-old Paul was essentially isolating him from his father, and that Gregory was reacting by allying with ten-year-old Stephanie against her mother.

This kind of schism threatens the entire family. Obviously, Gregory and Jane have some problem in their relationship, and the family alignments are working to drive them even further apart. The son and daughter are locked into unhealthy relationships that can inhibit their future growth and development. Each parent favors one child and consciously or unconsciously undermines that child's relationship with the other parent. When Gregory made an effort to reach out to Paul during a counseling session, Jane interrupted with a

Family Counseling Strategies for Establishing New Relationship Skills[18]

1. Training in Communication Skills	The counselor systematically helps family members to eliminate deficits in communication and develop effective new communication patterns by modeling the new skill, coaching family members, offering feedback, and having members rehearse skills during the session. Typically, the skills trained include listening, empathy, assertiveness, expressing personal emotions, talking about one's negative emotions, and expressing appreciation and positive support.
2. Training in Solving Problems	The counselor trains couples how to negotiate directly for desired behavior changes in their marital relationship. The skills taught include (1) how to define problems clearly, (2) how to admit to one's role in a problem, (3) how to focus on one problem at a time, (4) how to be specific about behaviors one wants to be changed, (5) how to paraphrase the partner's statements before expressing one's own ideas, (6) how to brainstorm possible solutions to mutually defined problems, (7) how to compromise
2. Training in Solving Problems *(Continued)*	appropriately, and (8) how to specify agreements for change.
3. Homework Assignments	The counselor assigns specific tasks to be accomplished in the home between family counseling sessions. These tasks focus on counseling goals pertaining to changing patterns of interaction in the family or restructuring boundaries in the family system.

sarcastic remark that goaded her husband into an argument with her. When Paul sided with his mother, Gregory retreated from the conversation and turned to Stephanie for sympathy and cooperation.

Where should the counselor begin in directing this family? Biblically and practically, the first change to seek is a firm alignment between the mother and the father. Once the bond in the core family relationship is strengthened, the counselor can deal with the other patterns. Watching the family interact, the counselor may offer an interpretation of what is going on and seek to build the relationship between the parents. After pointing out the splits in family relationships, the counselor may guide the family members to resolve the conflicts from a position of unity with one another.

Working with a Family Subsystem

This is also a good case for considering counseling for a family subsystem. After counseling the family as a whole, the basic problem was detected in the relationship between the husband and wife which indicated a need for some marriage counseling. Because of the unhealthy mother-son alliance evident in family sessions, the counselor may need to pull the husband and wife out separately where the unhealthy alliance is not operating to have a chance to work with the couple.

Here, the mother and father have a distant relationship, and if they each individually claim to have a personal relationship with Jesus Christ and if they agree to listen to Scripture, the counselor can say, "Now you've told me that you are followers of Jesus Christ and Jesus Himself said, 'My sheep listen to my voice'" (John 10:27). Then the Christian counselor can read them passages of Scripture about what should characterize their relationship. One might read to them some passages from the Sermon on the Mount which focus on interpersonal relationships and then exhort (2 Corinthians 9:5; 1 Thessalonians 5:14; 1 Timothy 6:2; Titus 2:15; Hebrews 3:13) and encourage (2 Chronicles 31:4; 35:2) them to apply those teachings.

You may need to warn them that they are at high risk for eventually dissolving their marriage. If they don't heal their relationship, the distance between the husband and wife will tempt one or the other of them to break up the marriage. In Scripture, warning usually means "to make known, to teach, to show something" (as in Matthew 3:7; Luke 3:7; 12:5) or to warn somebody ahead of time (Matthew 2:12, 22; Acts 10:22; Hebrews 8:5; 11:7; 12:25). This tactic may give the family some fresh insight into their family dynamics and they might respond, "Hey, that's right. This shouldn't be this way. We're not really showing love to one another."

The counselor can use 1 Corinthians 13 as a test by rephrasing the description of love and asking at each verse, "Love is patient. Is this the way your relationship is? Love is kind. Are you being kind here?" We have the assurance from Scripture itself that true Christians will respond to God's Word (Matthew 4:4; John 8:47; 12:47, 48; 14:10; 15:7).

Pastoral versus Nonpastoral Counseling

This particular counseling care also raises the issue of the advantages and disadvantages of pastoral counseling for being able to use this tactic of directing change. Holding the office of pastor-teacher in the church is a unique role to have in counseling a family. There are also certain advantages and disadvantages for a nonpastoral counselor, whether it be in a church counseling center or in the private practice office of a professional psychologist, psychiatrist, clinical social worker or other family counselor.

One of the advantages of being a pastoral counselor is that one has an authority relationship with the person in the church. The person being counseled, particularly the believer, usually recognizes the pastor's authority to teach, instruct, exhort, reprove, and otherwise direct changes. If the wife is a believer and the husband is not and she wants her husband to come with her for some pastoral counseling, the pastor, of course, has a different role with the believing wife than with the nonbelieving husband.

For some families, the fact that a pastor does not charge a fee is an advantage if the family is financially limited, or if an unbelieving spouse objects to a counselor who charges a fee, as a way to resist counseling help. On the other hand, for some families, the professional counselor charging a fee has an advantage because the person paying would experience the discomfort of "cognitive dissonance" if he or she did not value the counseling. "I'm paying a high price. This must be worth something," people in this situation tend to think. Therefore, they think twice before they discard the advice and refuse to change.

The psychological theory of cognitive dissonance is a bit complicated, but basically it says this: if a person has two dissonant cognitions—that is, two conflicting thoughts at the same time—the mind has the tendency to try to resolve the conflict by trying to dismiss one thought while believing the other one. If the counselee feels, "I don't have to be here. I don't want to follow this counseling," and yet the session is costing money, he or she is having two dissonant cognitions, "This is something I don't need and don't want and yet I'm paying for it." So, that person needs to resolve it one way or another, either by not coming to counseling anymore or by deciding that the counseling must be worth something and then trying to follow it and change problem behavior.

With the case of the mother-son and father-daughter alliances, the whole family was in a lot of pain, and they saw that they needed help. But at the same time, they had a lot invested in the family dynamic the way it was going. This made it difficult for them to shift. But, as an act of the will, they decided they wanted to come in and get help. In this case, when the counselor said, "I want to see the mother and father alone," they cooperated. The counselor pointed out some ways to strengthen their alliance as marriage partners and as co-parents. Then they followed through, but it required a period of time to learn some new patterns of interaction to replace old habits. It was not only a matter of their wills, but also a matter of learning new behaviors with the counselor's guidance.

But by far the most important aspect of this counseling situation was that the husband and wife developed a closer relationship with God that brought them closer to each other. Over the years, there had been so many different ways that this husband and wife had sinned against each other. The years of sinning against each other had taken a toll and had begun to disintegrate their marriage. The pastoral counselor can take proper advantage of his role as a spiritual leader in helping the couple forgive each other as he helps them understand and appropriate God's forgiveness of them.

From a biblical perspective, marriage was designed to have the spiritual and moral elements involved. If these are left out, then what the Christian counselor can do for a husband and wife and their relationships with their children is somewhat limited. At this point, a pastoral counselor could fittingly call the unbelieving family members to repentance over their sin and help them turn to Jesus Christ for forgiveness and salvation. A counselor can accomplish some things even if family members are not believers and refuse the gospel, but real and lasting progress is possible only to the extent that they learn to behave in ways that are consistent with sound psychological and biblical principles of relationships. The extent of change is potentially greater for the family members who have experienced a genuine conversion.

CHAPTER EIGHT

CHALLENGES IN FAMILY COUNSELING

A STUDENT IN DRIVER'S EDUCATION is typically required to study separately the rules of the road, how to use turn signals, ways to hold the steering wheel, skills in turning left and right, methods of parallel parking, and the like. At first, in the driver's training car, the student driver must attend to each of these component skills in driving. But eventually, the driver combines all this education and training into the ability to drive smoothly and safely to the desired destination without having to consciously think of all the steps in between, such as how far to turn the steering wheel, how hard to press the accelerator, how soon before an intersection to apply the brake, and so forth.

Just as the student of driving eventually performs the many

functions of driving largely unconsciously, the experienced family counselor maneuvers through the phases of counseling without having to consciously attend to many of the matters we have carefully isolated and dissected. Family counseling moves from the challenges of resistance in early sessions, through planning, through the middle stages oriented toward results, to the final session of termination when the counselor has successfully reached the intended goal of becoming obsolete for the family. Each of these phases is necessary and often demanding, but the counselor needs to be aware that many families find the transitions into and out of the counseling relationship particularly difficult.

HANDLING RESISTANCE TO COUNSELING

It is not unusual for some family members to be more motivated to receive help than others. Some may not only lack motivation but may actively resist the counseling process. Typically, at least one person in the family has asked for the family counseling, so usually resistance is coming from one or more of the members who did not ask for the counseling. The successful counselor recognizes resistance and deals with it. What are some signs of resistance and what should counselors do when they encounter resistance?

Recognizing Resistance

Resistance can come out in various forms. A child, for example, may refuse to talk during the family sessions. Resistance can take the form of excessive silence, even if a family member does talk occasionally. A teenager may flatly refuse to attend the session. Or the resistance might be more subtle than that. The teenager may be showing up and participating minimally, but insisting, "I really don't want to talk about heavy topics in front of my parents." This statement indicates a willingness to deal only with superficiality.

In other instances, just the opposite happens: excessive talking becomes a form of resistance. As a counselor, you feel that you are being filibustered by family members who are just filling up the time with chatter. Some counselors refer to this as "verbal diarrhea."

171

Evasiveness is another form of resistance. A family member may offer superficial answers or make remarks that are off the topic. A similar tactic is to avoid telling the truth by constantly pulling the counselor's leg. One time a thirteen-year-old boy in the first family counseling session would give an obviously silly or wrong answer to any question I asked. His mother would say, "Come on, Charles, be honest. How can the doctor help you if you're not honest?" This was the way Charles resisted the whole process. It wasn't his idea to come in for counseling, and he wasn't asking for any help.

Resistance may be either direct or indirect. Direct resistance is openly expressed, whereas indirect resistance hides beneath a feigned compliance. The counselor must not be fooled by appearances. The person who says, "Oh, sure, I'll do that," but never follows through with the promised behavior is resisting change just as effectively as the person who yells, "No, I won't!"

Indirect resistance may take the form of manipulating family members during the counseling session. For instance, the parents may act in a phony way, putting themselves forward as Mr. and Mrs. Nice. Although they do not relate this way at home, during counseling they resist honest dealing with their problems by being overly kind and deferring: "What do you think, dear?" Sometimes adolescents will use their dress and appearance to let their parents and counselor know that they view the whole endeavor as a joke.

The parents may state that a child or teenager is so obviously the family's problem that individual counseling is the whole answer, making it unnecessary to go through the inconvenience of getting the whole family together. In some cases, this is a form of resistance to family counseling. There may well be a need for individual counseling, but this does not automatically do away with the need for also using family sessions.

Some families arrive late, miss their appointments without calling to cancel, or excessively call to reschedule appointments.

Others neglect to pay their bills for counseling. Several times I have had counseling clients with insurance coverage who did not pay their bill but asked me to fill in some detailed insurance forms. The insurance company reimbursed them months later for thousands of dollars, and they never paid me. The insurance payment went straight to them, I sent them my bill as they agreed, but they just ignored it.

Once resistance is identified, the question arises: What can the counselor do about it? Do you throw up your hands, leave your counseling office and give up? If so, that would certainly be the end of that problem, right? But seriously, there are several principles to follow when encountering resistance to family counseling.

1. Set and enforce ground rules.
2. Identify and deal with underlying anxieties.
3. Emphasize personal responsibility.

Setting Ground Rules

Some experienced family counselors make certain rules in advance to forestall commonly encountered manifestations of resistance. For example, the rule might be that if any family member is not present, then there will be no family counseling session. If the family and the counselor have agreed to this in the first family meeting and one person fails to show up at a later meeting, then that session is simply rescheduled for another time. This puts some family pressure on that missing family member: "Here we had this agreed-upon appointment time, Mom rescheduled her hair appointment, Terry skipped a birthday party he was invited to, Dad took off work an hour early to come, but Billy wasn't here." He "forgot" the appointment.

In other families, the members all attend, but one member rarely speaks. At least that person's attendance is one step in a positive direction. When you deal with families with multiple problems, you must often be satisfied with small steps of progress. In this case, the counselor might express appreciation that all family members attended the session, and make a statement to the effect that the family will benefit the most from the sessions if everyone participates in talking.

In some cases, the counselor decides the family needs counseling as a whole. Or perhaps another counselor is dealing with an individual in the family. An appropriate rule for this situation would be that all counseling sessions will deal with the family together. Family members may express resistance to family counseling by requesting an individual appointment. If they do, the counselor clarifies the rule: that is, that the counselor will meet with the whole family only. Some people skip family sessions in hopes that the counselor will call them in for an individual appointment. Other counselors don't make such a rule, and they'll go ahead and meet with the family members who show up.

Occasionally, everyone shows up but someone says that he or she does not want to meet with the family and would rather meet the counselor alone. This individual might ask to meet alone for part of the session: "Let me have the first fifteen minutes." If this seems to be a form of resistance, the counselor can clarify the reasons for not seeing people individually and then let the whole family discuss that as an issue.

Another tactic is to ask the family member directly about the resistance. You might call the absent member to ask why he or she didn't attend the session, and point out the pattern of absences. Or if the resister is there, ask why he or she is arriving late every week and deal with the resistance directly as a counseling issue. You may need to confront an issue like this, deal with it briefly, and then move on.

Dealing with Underlying Anxieties

Try to assess the reason for the resistance. Some resistance is conscious and the person may have certain emotions that underlie the resistance. For example, people who fear rejection or criticism often decide not to open their mouths to say anything. People may be ashamed of their behavior and feel reluctant to talk about it in front of the counselor. They might not trust the counselor. It may take several counseling sessions to develop trust in the counselor. By asking individuals about their resistance and by asking other family members about what it means, you can assess how aware they are of such motives. Other kinds of resistance are unconscious. In other words, the person himself couldn't tell you exactly why he's resisting the counseling process. In this case, it may take a longer time to draw out those dynamics.

If you've assessed that the reason for resistance is a lack of trust or the presence of fear, you may want to focus on the strengths of the individual and draw them out by talking about less threatening topics at first until trust can be built up over time. It helps to get a person talking if you deal with familiar, everyday topics at first, show that you have a sense of humor, and demonstrate that you're not going to sit there as a stern judge looking for every flaw in order to hammer away at people and humiliate them. Often for families with younger children, you might bring toys into the room, and encourage them to talk while they play. Sometimes when I counsel families with children at the university hospital where I work, I'll take the children downstairs to the canteen area and buy them a soda pop or something from the food machines in order to develop a little rapport. It is less threatening for them to start talking while we walk down and back.

If there is an abusive relationship between the parent and child, the counselor may decide to have an individual session with the child or teenager. You may suggest meeting with each family member individually to develop a rapport with them before getting together for a family session. Counselors need to improvise in many ways. Be alert and sensitive to people's feelings. It becomes important, not only to have empathy, but to demonstrate empathy by what you say.

Sometimes resistance can be cleared up by just explaining more about what you're trying to accomplish in the family counseling setting, why it's important, and what's in it for them. If some family members are initially resistant, or not being serious, you might ask them to explain how this family counseling process could be helpful to them. After they and the family discuss that, there may be greater cooperation.

The family counselor may need to extend forgiveness to someone who is sabotaging the counseling. Demonstrate a Christ-like character that communicates that you are not going to hold grudges. You may even say, "I forgive you. You're taking up a lot of our time, you're not being serious, and sometimes you don't show up. But I forgive you and I'm willing to work with you if you're able to change that pattern."

Usually I see more resistance in the first session where there are a number of family members very apprehensive about what this process is going to be like. Some people's only conception of counseling has been gleaned from watching the old "Bob Newhart Show" on TV. They may have a number of different stereotypes of counseling, but once they discover that you are a real person and you are trying to be helpful to them, they often open up.

The counselor should avoid power struggles and avoid the misconception that you might take over parenting authority or responsibility, which would set up a form of power struggle. Give the family the opportunity to ask questions, and frankly answer their questions. Many times Christians will want to know where you stand on certain issues. After they ask you a few questions and see that you take a biblical approach, then they become comfortable with you.

Sometimes parents will come in and say, "Yes, I'm willing to do whatever I can, no matter what the sacrifice, to help Tony get better." Then they'll turn to the child and say, "Well, now Tony, you tell the counselor, dear, what the problem is. Come on, talk now. There's no reason to be afraid. You know you can be completely open and honest and say whatever you want. We can handle anything you might say. Even if you feel like saying some mean and angry things about Mommy and Daddy, that's just fine. Maybe that would make you feel better. Just say whatever you want."

While the surface message of what they're saying is this, "You can be open and say whatever you want," the hidden message is, "You'd better give a good impression of our family." They insist, "You can say anything you feel," but really mean the opposite.

So, Tony replies in a weak, halfhearted way, "Well, there is really nothing I can think of that's a problem." Or, "Nothing is bothering me today." With this safe response, Tony has not risked saying the wrong thing or anything that could be considered disloyal. He has avoided bringing criticism on himself, and he has managed to avoid the impression of being inept or mentally disturbed.

After further questions, Tony eventually makes a vague

statement about the marital conflict and how it is bothering him. Father quickly changes the subject, Tony's sister starts to giggle nervously, and with a dumfounded look, the mother dramatically places her hand on her forehead and explodes with something like, "See what a trying problem Tony is. He is constantly embarrassing me like this in public. See, I told you that I have a very sick and troubled child."

Although each parent says, "I'm willing to do whatever I can to solve this problem," the parents are in fact resistant to considering the possibility that they themselves have a problem they need to face. Instead, they pin all the problems on another family member. In this case, it is helpful for the counselor to suggest that the problem does not appear to reside with an individual only, but resides in the family system—that is, in relationships. The counselor then proceeds to ask each family member to describe the *family relationships* that are occurring.

Emphasizing Personal Responsibility

Often resistance boils down to a matter of the will. When certain family members decide not to go along with the counseling agenda, then clarify that it is their responsibility and no one can actually force them to cooperate. You must be willing in such cases to do the best you can and leave it at that. Provide a process for them to grow and to change. Help them to see biblical reasons for changing. Confront them with biblical principles. Call them and ask them to change their behavior pattern. But in the final analysis then you have to leave it with them to make their decision.

Dealing with passive-aggressive persons is extremely difficult because they won't debate you. Instead, they'll agree with everything you say and promise to follow any recommendation. But they may not carry it out. They "forget" to, or find other reasons later for noncompliance. You may need to confront the passive-aggressive person regarding the habitual incongruity between his or her statements and behavior. Explain that often actions speak louder than words, and that you realize from the outset that you cannot force someone to be cooperative. Each individual has a free will.

Many counselors see it as a challenge to try to manipulate a person or family to do what they're supposed to do, but I question the wisdom of such an attitude. A counselor can only be available as a resource, as a help, making the relationship process more explicit, and pointing out passive-aggressive behavior patterns. Bringing these patterns out into the open can sometimes take a lot of the punch out of being passive-aggressive for a family member. The other people in the family start talking about this type of behavior as being passive-aggressive, and this may motivate the person to change.

Sometimes it is effective to get a clearer contract with resistant persons. Ask what their view of the family is, what's going on, where they see problems, and what goals they want to work on. In this way, you negotiate a contract for coming to counseling.

An adolescent may insist, "There is no problem, so if they would just leave me alone, I'd be just fine. I don't need to come to this counseling session. I don't like this."

The counselor can respond, "Well, the fact is the family sees it differently and they are not going to leave you alone. Since you're part of the family, what is it that you want to do? We're here to help you get what you want if it's something appropriate."

In many cases of resistance, the family will just drop out of counseling. But this is not inevitable. You don't have to give up. You can identify resistance and you can try a number of these strategies to deal with it. If you can build a relationship during the first session by being as nonthreatening as possible, then hopefully they will come back for more sessions and be less resistant.

In rare cases, I have discontinued family counseling myself even though the family did not ask to terminate. At times I am forced to conclude that it's just not a workable situation. It would be a waste of their time and a waste of my time to proceed with a resistant family member. If there is an extremely resistant pattern, I may tell a family, "Call back in a month or two if you change your mind, but at the moment, I don't see a reason to continue meeting."

In such a case, a counselor may choose to work only with the receptive people in the family. Although this is not ideal, it can be preferable to continuing counseling which is greatly disrupted by some family member who is fouling up every session and undermining your objectives.

"Good Daddy/Mean Mother"

Some forms of resistance can influence the therapeutic goal for some families. This was the case for a family with a thirteen-year-old girl, Ellen, who was 4' 11" and weighed 262 pounds.[1] She was a middle-school student and the oldest of four children. Ellen's mother complained that she just could not control her daughter's eating habits. The more the girl continued to eat, the more her mother was frustrated. She tried all kinds of methods to get Ellen to diet. She was worried about the girl's health.

The father was an independent businessman and ran his own little bakery in a shopping mall. Not only was the father overweight, but the mother, a part-time bookkeeper, was thirty pounds overweight, many of the aunts and uncles were somewhat plump and, to a lesser extent, the three younger sons were heavier than average. The mother insisted that she had tried all the advice of her doctor to get this girl to lose weight, but nothing had worked. So she urgently wanted Ellen hospitalized.

The girl and her mother fought over discipline in general and eating restrictions in particular. The family had no regular mealtimes at home, and each individual raided the refrigerator and kitchen cupboards at will. So Ellen felt singled out by her mother's restrictions on the times she could eat and the particular foods she could have. Mother complained that Ellen would lock herself in her room after arguing over eating sweets. After these conflicts, Ellen would often pout in her room until her father came home. When he arrived, Ellen would hysterically sob and insist that her mother had been insensitive and cruel. Without asking any further questions of Ellen or his wife, the father would side with Ellen and tell his wife, "You're being unreasonable again with Ellen." Then he would remove whatever the mother's discipline was and then typically he'd take Ellen out for pizza, a sundae, or a pastry at his store to "make up for her mean mother."

The husband/wife relationship was not only poor and remote but had lacked physical intimacy for about two years. The mother had tried to get the family into family counseling a number of times, but the father had always refused. He had also resisted the suggestion of marriage counseling and individual psychotherapy. The father related to the children as the jovial "nice guy" and the mother related to the children as the disciplinarian, but father and mother essentially ignored each other to avoid arguments. In response to the conflict in the mother/daughter relationship, the father was playing a "good daddy" role, indulging the children and usually not disciplining them.

Ellen was admitted to a hospital with an adolescent psychiatric ward and she stayed for twelve months to participate in nutritional control, milieu therapy, individual psychotherapy with a psychiatrist, and family counseling by a hospital chaplain. During the first two months in this controlled setting of calorie restrictions, Ellen lost thirty-seven pounds. At the end of seven months she had lost eighty-three pounds, and by ten months, she had lost a full 102 pounds, reaching a weight of 160 pounds.

At first, when family counseling began, the father continued to resist. The mother and other children came in and described some of the typical family situations: when mother tried to tell Ellen to stop eating, Ellen would scream back, hit at her, swear, throw household items, and threaten to throw more things if she didn't get her sweets. She talked possessively about her sweets. She insisted she had to have her candy. Ellen would often stop after school by her father's bakery store and he'd tell her to help herself. He also gave her money to buy candy in adjacent stores in the mall. Sometimes she would stay there until her father closed shop and they would go out to eat before going home.

The family counselor noted the father's continued absence and asked the family what they could do about it. The family agreed that they would each individually ask him to come with them in the most positive way they could think of. Finally, the father came in for a family counseling session. The counselor asked the father, "Why is it that you seem to give in to so many of the demands of your daughter? It looks like you might be giving in to every demand your children make on you. Your wife is trying to resist some of their demands, but you have a different approach. Can you explain that?" The father replied that he never felt comfortable saying no to any of his children because he was afraid he might lose their love.

Then the mother admitted her resentment and anger toward the father for his indulgent relationship with the children. She explained that this led her to feel isolated, powerless, and helpless. The father indulged his children and experienced a superficial closeness to them. This cast the mother in the role of the legendary wicked mother figure of the fairy tales, because she was the one placing demands on the children. She felt very depressed over her sense of loss of control, and she admitted that the reason she wanted Ellen hospitalized was to separate her from the family, not only so she could deal with her weight problem, but for relief at home.

Actually, it was working out this way. Ellen was losing weight. But the family counseling sessions revealed that while she was in the hospital, her father further developed his seductive-like pattern with her. He telephoned her at different times, told her how much he loved her, and sympathized with her about what a "mean mother" she had who would talk the doctors into putting her in the hospital. He sent her flowers. He sent her candy, even though she was on a diet in the hospital. When he came down to visit her in the hospital, the nurse would inform her of his arrival in the lobby, but she would keep him waiting for about fifteen to twenty minutes. This deliberate delay made her ultimate appearance more dramatic and appealing to the father. So there emerged, in the family session, a picture of this kind of unhealthy relationship going on between the father and daughter.

After coming to that one family session, he then resisted several other sessions. But even in his absence, the family continued to focus on this issue. Eventually this family was able to convince the father to come in and he was able to gain some insight into his immature pattern with Ellen. Instead of being overprotective and indulging her, he learned how to help her to overcome her self-indulgent, destructive pattern. She was discharged from the hospital after twelve months, weighing 140 pounds. She continued individual psychotherapy to help her maintain her weight and the family counseling continued.

Eventually, over a long period of time, counseling was successful. Two years later, Ellen had maintained her weight at 140 and had a much better view of herself. She gradually developed a better relationship with her mother. Marriage counseling was necessary for the mother and the father and their relationship did improve. Finally, months and years later the father developed a more realistic and normal relationship with his daughter.

This case study powerfully illustrates that the very existence of resistance to counseling can be a core part of what's wrong with the family. A major factor underlying a family problem can manifest itself as resistance to the counseling process as well.

ENDING THE COUNSELING SESSION

While some family members may be reluctant to participate or talk, and even be eager to get the family session over with, other families pose the opposite problem for the counselor.

With some people, it is very, very difficult to end a counseling session. One way to prevent this problem is to make the time limits clear at the beginning of the counseling session. If you start a ninety-minute family counseling session at 4:00 P.M., you could say, "Our appointment will end at 5:30." If you have a particular family for whom it has been difficult to end a session, five minutes before the end of the session you might say, "Now we have five minutes left of your session and I want to summarize where we've come up to this point and take the final steps here for today." You might even schedule their next appointment six or seven minutes before the end of the session and then go into the summary.

But some families will still seem to filibuster you. If they continue talking past your announcement of the end of the session, you may need to get up out of your chair, motion for them to follow you, and start walking out the door. Usually if they're still talking, they'll keep on talking and follow you out the door. Fortunately, most families will take a hint if you look at your watch and say, "We have just a minute or two left here."

Most professional counselors work with families for a fifty- to ninety-minute session. Some believe that if you counsel for less time than this you might not really get much accomplished, but it really depends on what the task is for the session. Many pastors don't have many hours left during the day after they prepare sermons, do visitation, and attend meetings. They have only a limited number of hours during the week to devote to counseling. But with an entire family, there are more dynamics going on, and the counselor needs to spend a longer time in a session than is required for individual counseling. But work with families is sometimes more efficient than dealing with individuals and may take fewer sessions to get things accomplished.

Often there is some advantage to a husband and wife cocounselor team. There are some husband and wife counseling teams that are quite effective, but that requires working well together in a counseling situation. One advantage to this type of cocounseling is the opportunity to model a positive relationship.

PHASING OUT FAMILY COUNSELING

We certainly haven't discussed everything you might possibly need to know about family counseling, but the references in the appendixes to this book will provide a start toward continuous learning about this challenging type of counseling. We are now ready to discuss some things to keep in mind in the process of terminating family counseling.

Ideally, the counselor and the family together decide that the goals of counseling have been accomplished and that it is time to end or terminate the counseling process. In practice, many families drop out of counseling by simply failing to make an appointment and declining to schedule any further sessions. It is preferable to raise termination issues well in advance, so that termination can proceed in a more orderly way.

Sometimes a family will get to the end of the school year,

and find that they have reached some short-term goals. Then they take a vacation from counseling over the summer and start up again in September to work on some other goals.

You may have a family request counseling in a crisis situation. After you have worked together to resolve the major crisis, there may be many other things to be attended to, but the family's goal was to just live through the crisis. In such a case, you can suggest that they call you if they have some other goals they want to work on. If you let the family decide when they want to come back again, then they may have increased their motivation the next time they come in: They decided to try to solve some problem on their own, found it didn't work, and then came in motivated for counseling.

From time to time before making the decision to phase out counseling, the counselor can review with the family what progress has been made toward different goals and what still needs to be done. When a member of the family asks if it is time to end counseling, it is a good time to review the family's progress or lack of progress and what might continue to constitute a need for further sessions. In determining whether a family is ready to terminate, you can ask a number of questions:

1. Compared to when they first came in, is this family more successful in applying biblical principles in their family relationships?

2. Have both the presenting problem and what you determined to be the underlying problem been satisfactorily resolved? For example, if family members were scapegoating a certain member, have they ceased scapegoating?

3. Has the family developed new and more loving patterns of communication?

4. Has the family developed more adequate interaction patterns to replace the maladaptive forms of relating and communicating? For example, are family members making more clear and helpful statements to one another with explicit meaning?

5. Are the family's communication methods more conducive to solving daily problems now rather than generating conflict by dealing with surface issues, or by evading the problem? If counseling has been effective, the family has

learned how to solve problems together in the counseling session, and has gained experience in defining a problem, setting a goal, and working together toward a solution. Hopefully, they transfer that process out of the counseling time, do it more and more in between counseling sessions, and then report during counseling session, "Well, when we had this problem that came up on Tuesday night, Billy said this, Susie said that, we sat down to talk about it together, and we came up with a solution." When the counselor sees this happen, the family is getting closer to termination.

6. Are the family members forgiving one another more?

7. Are they bearing one another's burdens more effectively?

8. Is their family life more harmonious on a regular basis? Are they accepting their differences? Are they able to promote the individual development and maturation of each family member?

9. Are they setting clear, reasonable, and scriptural limits and then living by those limits in terms of the children obeying regularly and the parents carrying out their responsibilities in discipline?

10. Are the family members individually aware of and accepting of their responsibilities and their roles? Is the father taking a loving, involved leadership role? Is the mother assuming her proper role in disciplining the children and being appropriately submissive to her husband?

After you have ended your family counseling, you might need to continue with one or more family members with individual counseling. Other families are so chaotic that to get any sense of accomplishment at all for the family, you may need to set some short-term goals to accomplish, address a short list of their problems, and then terminate counseling even though they still have a lot of problems. You may decide to not address all the issues that may be involved. Terminating counseling depends upon what you had aimed at doing. You compare how the family is functioning now to what your initial goals were. If you fail to set goals at the outset, it will be hard to know when to end because you will not have a clear sense of what has been accomplished.

Sometimes the counselor might recommend just terminating counseling outright. In other cases, it is wiser to phase out sessions gradually. After meeting once a week, you may shift to scheduling a session once every two weeks and then later only once a month, until you finally stop counseling. In family counseling, the number of sessions runs between eight to twenty for the vast majority of families. No family is going to leave counseling problem-free, but it should be leaving with better, more adaptive functioning and a greater ability to work on problems when they do come up. Hopefully, family members have discovered psychological and spiritual resources to resolve their problems in the home, using effective strategies learned in counseling.

APPENDIXES

Appendix 1   Models of Family Counseling

Family therapists and family counselors distinguish their work from individual psychotherapy or counseling and have developed a variety of theoretical models of clinical practice. As noted in chapter 7, research has established that the majority of family therapists consider themselves "eclectic" in their approach, drawing their therapeutic approaches from a variety of models. As an introductory overview of family counseling, this book has also essentially taken this common eclectic approach, integrating various family counseling methods under the conceptual framework provided by the final authority of Scripture on matters of family relationships.

However, the reader who is involved in counseling families on a regular basis will need to consult more advanced and specialized academic articles and books on family therapy to meet the challenges of working with a diverse number of family problems. This appendix provides a very brief introduction to the spectrum of family counseling models which can be pursued in greater detail by consulting various books listed in Appendix 2.

There currently exists no set of widely agreed-upon techniques of family counseling or therapy. Instead, counseling approaches draw upon psychodynamic theories, communication theories, structural theory, and behavior theories. Each of these four approaches to describing family interaction will be briefly described together with examples of family therapists who have derived intervention techniques from each approach.

INTERVENTIONS BASED ON FAMILY PSYCHODYNAMIC THEORIES

The psychodynamic view of individual behavior focuses upon the conflicts among psychological forces within a person to explain his or her motives and emotions. Applied to family relationships, the psychodynamic approach stresses the "interlocking pathology" among family members, whose inner psychological lives and conflicts are entangled with other family members. Psychodynamic theories are largely based upon psychoanalysis, which assumes that the emotional disturbance of an individual is developed in relationships and that the relationship with a therapist is the most effective way to correct that disturbance.

Nathan Ackerman's Biopsychosocial Therapy

Ackerman (1966) diagnosed the dynamic relationships among family members. He assessed the emotional currents underlying family problems, and he viewed the family therapist's role as offering "reeducation," "reorganization," and "resolution" of conflict. Thus, he sought to assist family members to get in better touch with their emotions, thoughts, and behavior.

Murray Bowen's Family Systems Therapy

Bowen (1978) viewed himself as a "coach" who actively helped individual "players" and their "team" (their family) to perform up to their capacity. Focusing on the family system, he attempted to change its usual triangulations and to help family members differentiate themselves from the "undifferentiated family ego mass." He typically focused on the marital couple, having them speak to him rather than to one another, attempting to "defuse" emotions from thinking. He sought to remain neutral, calm, and unentangled in the marital conflict. He had each family member focus upon his or her part in family relationship problems.

INTERVENTIONS BASED ON FAMILY COMMUNICATIONS THEORY

Rather than focusing upon internal psychological processes, the communication theorists view family conflicts as relationship problems which are manifested in faulty communication. All behavior is viewed as communication, and mixed, contradictory, faulty, and double-bind messages are viewed as central factors in family problems. The therapist observes not only verbal content but also nonverbal communication by tone of voice, inflection, posture, gestures, and other "body language." From this approach, various new therapeutic techniques have been developed, including brief family therapy which is a direct, pragmatic approach to helping families adapt by making their communication more honest, congruent, and effective.

Virginia Satir's Conjoint Family Therapy

Satir (1967; 1972) focuses on the ways family members have developed communication with one another, and she seeks to help them comprehend and overcome their communication problems by teaching them specific communication skills. She emphasizes the critical importance of intimacy in family relationships, and her counseling approach promotes communication of needs in ways that promote self-worth. Satir's technique is active, direct, and practical as she attempts to help the family grow, change, and cope. She provides a model of direct, clear, congruent communication, and assists the process of change as a facilitator.

Jay Haley's Problem-Solving Therapy

A pioneer practitioner and author in family therapy, Haley (1963; 1971; 1976) focuses upon the power aspects of relationships and prescribes tactics for remaining in control and for actively directing families to make changes in their patterns of behavior. Strongly rejecting the psychodynamic explanation for symptoms (such as anxiety attacks, depressive episodes, phobias, or alcohol drinking spells), Haley views symptoms as interpersonal tactics used by one individual to control the definition of his or her relationship with another person. As a therapist, Haley designs methods for encouraging a person to develop other strategies for defining the relationship. This renders the symptoms obsolete so they can be abandoned. He also emphasizes the power maneuvers used by therapists and patients with one another, and advocates that family therapists should use strategies to stay in charge and to direct family changes.

INTERVENTIONS BASED ON STRUCTURAL FAMILY THEORY

Structural family theory focuses upon relationships among various family subsystems, the family boundaries, and the capacity of a family to readjust to changes brought about by developmental stages. Primarily developed by Minuchin (1974a), this structuralist theory emphasizes the active wholeness of the family unit and how this is governed by certain organized arrangements. Family interactions are observed as clues to underlying organization or structure. Thus, in contrast to family communication theories, it is said that the structuralists are concerned primarily with *how* individuals communicate in the family rather than with *what* is communicated. Structural family theory includes such concepts as enmeshment, disengagement, family "map," and homeostasis.

Salvador Minuchin's Structural Therapy

As a therapist, Minuchin (1974a; 1974b) enters a family, affiliates and adapts to it, then designs interventions to rearrange the organization of a family, hoping to restructure the system in such a way that the family then substitutes more functional styles of relating. He restructures the family by confronting and challenging dysfunctional patterns that maintain undesired behaviors. His family therapy techniques have been described as "innovative," "deliberatively manipulative," "dramatic," "theatrical," and "unconventional" (Goldenberg & Goldenberg, 1980, pp. 180–81). His therapy tactics increase stress on the family, sometimes to the point of precipitating a family crisis by throwing the family homeostasis off balance. This, in turn, sets the scene for changing the family structure, establishing more appropriate ways for family members to relate to one another. He views pathological symptoms as embedded in a problematic family organization which needs to be restructured in family therapy.

INTERVENTIONS BASED ON FAMILY BEHAVIOR THEORY

Maladaptive family patterns are explained in terms of learning principles by the family behavior theorists. Positive and negative reinforcement, operant conditioning, shaping, modeling, extinction, and other learning procedures are systematically applied to modify family problems. A behavioral analysis requires careful operational definitions of problem behaviors, systematic observations, and reliable recording of behaviors and the stimulus events associated with them. This behavioral assessment clarifies the contingencies maintaining problem behaviors. Therapeutic goals are then agreed upon and the therapist guides families to alter reinforcement contingencies.

Gerald Patterson's Social Learning Therapy

Patterson (1971) focuses upon training parents to use effective behavior management skills in helping their children learn and perform adaptive behavior patterns. Based upon extensive research with problem children and their families, he has formulated specific recommended procedures for such things as teaching parents how to observe child behavior, record a baseline, specify behavior they want to change, or negotiate reinforcement contracts. Supported by many federal research grants, Patterson has demonstrated the effectiveness of this behavior approach.

Richard Stuart's Operant-Interpersonal Therapy

Stuart (1976) has reported his extensive research on therapy interventions for couples with marital discord. He attempts to help the spouses develop the best relationship they can. He developed an eight-stage model of the treatment process which is designed to accelerate positive changes in marital behavior. He advocates negotiating behavioral contracts between spouses and teaching couples more effective decision-making strategies. He teaches couples to measure progress with self-assessments at four-month intervals and institute new objectives for additional changes in the relationship.

Robert Liberman's Contingency Contracting

Liberman (1972) also attempts to reprogram reinforcement contingencies that operate in a family by drawing up contingency contracts between various family members, who agree upon specific exchanges of positively rewarding behaviors. Liberman negotiates goals in behavioral terms, then guides the family to change the existing contingencies of reinforcement operating in the family to increase adaptive and decrease maladaptive behaviors. Liberman emphasizes the role of the therapist in relating to the family and incorporates a systems perspective. He has developed the technique of "contingency contracting" which involves identifying rewards for other family members and for oneself, setting priorities on rewards, empathizing, setting costs on providing rewards, and bargaining.

OTHER INTERVENTION MODELS

A variety of other models for family counseling have been developed by other independent therapists. For example, Gerald Zuk (1971) has developed a "Triadic-Based Family Therapy" approach in which he acts to control the go-between process among family members in an attempt to change chronic maladaptive relationship patterns.

John Bell (1975) developed "Family Group Therapy" based upon the social psychology of small group behavior. Bell facilitates problem solving and family decision making by serving as a group process leader.

H. P. Laquer (1976) developed "multiple family therapy" in which groups of four or more families are seen together by a therapist who acts as a facilitator.

Appendix 2 contains primary references to the above family counseling models and also includes recent handbooks and textbooks on family counseling which provide more specialized information on a variety of intervention techniques.

Appendix 2   Selected References on Family Counseling Methods

Ackerman, N. W. *Treating the Troubled Family.* New York: Basic Books, 1966.

Alexander, James, and Parsons, Bruce V. *Functional Family Therapy.* Monterey, Calif.: Brooks/Cole Publishing Company, 1982.

Anderson, Herbert. *The Family and Pastoral Care.* Philadelphia: Fortress Press, 1984.

Bell, J. E. *Family Therapy.* New York: Jason Aronson, 1975.

Bowen, M. *Family Therapy in Clinical Practice.* New York: Jason Aronson, 1978.

Bross, Allon, ed. *Family Therapy: Principles of Strategic Practice.* New York: Guilford Press, 1982.

Christensen, Oscar C., and Schramski, Thomas G., eds. *Adlerian Family Counseling: A Manual for Counselor, Educator and Psychotherapist.* Minneapolis: Educational Media Corporation, 1983.

Doherty, William J., and Baird, Macaran A. *Family Therapy and Family Medicine: Toward the Primary Care of Families.* New York: Guilford Press, 1983.

Framo, James L. *Explorations in Marital and Family Therapy.* New York: Springer Publishing Company, 1982.

Goldenberg, Irene, and Goldenberg, Herbert. *Family Therapy: An Overview.* Monterey, Calif.: Brooks/Cole Publishing Company, 1980.

Group for the Advancement of Psychiatry, The Committee on the Family. *Treatment of Families in Conflict: The Clinical Study of Family Process.* New York: Science House, 1970.

Gurman, Alan S., ed. *Questions and Answers in the Practice of Family Therapy.* New York: Brunner-Mazel Publishers, 1981.

Gurman, Alan S., and Kniskern, David P., eds. *Handbook of Family Therapy.* New York: Brunner-Mazel Publishers, 1981.

Haley, J., ed. *Changing Families.* New York: Grune & Stratton, 1971.

———. *Strategies of Psychotherapy.* New York: Grune & Stratton, 1963.

———. *Problem-Solving Therapy.* San Francisco: Jossey-Bass, 1976.

Hesselgrave, David J. *Counseling Cross-Culturally.* Grand Rapids: Baker Book House, 1984.

L'Abate, Luciano. *The Handbook of Family Psychology and Therapy.* 2 vols. Dorsey Professional Books, 1986.

Lange, Alfred, and van der Hart, Onno. *Directive Family Therapy.* New York: Brunner/Mazel Publishers, 1983.

Laquer, H. P. "Multiple Family Therapy." In *Family Therapy*, ed. P. J. Guerin. New York: Gardner Press, 1976.

Liberman, R. P. Behavioral Methods in Group and Family Therapy. *Seminars in Psychiatry*, 4 (1972): 145–56.

Lucas, Leon, and Goldberg, Ruth L. *Fundamentals of Family Counseling: A Primer on Learning and Teaching a Family-Focused Approach.* Northbrook, Ill.: Whitehall Company Publishers, 1969.

Minirth, Frank; Meier, Paul; Wichern, Frank; Brewer, Bill; and Skipper States. *The Workaholic and His Family.* Grand Rapids: Baker Book House, 1981.

Minuchin, S. *Families and Family Therapy.* Cambridge, Mass.: Harvard University Press, 1974(a).

———. "Structural Family Therapy." In *American Handbook of Psychiatry II*, 2d ed., S. Arietti and G. Kaplan, eds. New York: Basic Books, 1974(b).

Patterson, G. R. *Families.* Champaign, Ill.: Research Press, 1971.

Sauber, S. Richard; L'Abate, Luciano; and Weeks, Gerald R. *Family Therapy: Basic Concepts and Terms.* Rockville, Md.: Aspen Systems Corporation, 1985.

Satir, Virginia. *Conjoint Family Therapy.* Palo Alto, Calif.: Science and Behavior Books, 1967.

———. *Peoplemaking.* Palo Alto, Calif.: Science and Behavior Books, 1972.

Schulman, Gerda L. *Family Therapy: Teaching, Learning, Doing.* Washington, D.C.: University Press of America, 1982.

Stewart, Charles William. *The Minister as Family Counselor.* Nashville: Abingdon, 1979.

Stuart, R. B. "An Operant Interpersonal Program for Couples." In *Treating Relationships,* D. H. L. Olson, ed. Lake Mills, Iowa: Graphic, 1976.

Thorman, George. *Family Therapy: A Handbook.* Los Angeles: Western Psychological Services, 1975.

Tymchuk, Alexander J. *Parent and Family Therapy: An Integrated Approach to Family Interventions.* New York: S. P. Medical and Scientific Books, 1979.

Wynn, J. C. *Family Therapy in Pastoral Ministry.* San Francisco: Harper and Row, 1982.

Zuk, G. H. *Family Therapy.* New York: Human Sciences Press, 1971.

Appendix 3   Selected References on Family Relationships and Prevention

Arnold, L. Eugene, ed. *Parents, Children, and Change.* Lexington, Mass.: Lexington Books, 1985.

Bellah, Robert N.; Madsen, Richard; Sullivan, William M.; Swidler, N.; and Tipton, Steven. *Habits of the Heart: Individualism and Commitment in American Life.* Berkeley: University of California Press, 1985.

Berger, Brigitt, and Berger, Peter L. *The War Over the Family: Capturing the Middle Ground.* Garden City, N.Y.: Anchor Press/ Doubleday, 1983.

Campbell, D. Ross. *How to Really Love Your Child.* Wheaton, Ill.: Victor Books, 1977.

————. *How to Really Love Your Teenager.* Wheaton, Ill.: Victor Books, 1981.

Caplow, T. *All Faithful People: Change and Continuity in Middletown's Religion.* Minneapolis: University of Minnesota Press, 1983.

Curran, Dolores. *Traits of a Healthy Family: Fifteen Traits Commonly Found in Healthy Families by Those that Work with Them.* Minneapolis: Winston Press, 1983.

Dillow, Joseph C. *Solomon on Sex.* Nashville: Thomas Nelson, 1977.

Edelstein, Barry A., and Michelson, Larry, eds. *Handbook of Prevention.* New York: Plenum Publishing Co., 1986.

Figley, C., and McCubbin, H. *Stress on the Family. Coping with Normative Transitions* (vol. 1) and *Coping with Catastrophe* (vol. 2). New York: Brunner-Mazel, 1983.

Guernsey, Dennis B. *A New Design for Family Ministry.* Elgin, Ill.: David C. Cook, 1982.

Hancock, Maxine, and Mains, Karen. *Child Sexual Abuse.* Wheaton, Ill.: Harold Shaw, 1987.

Howell, John C. *Church and Family Growing Together.* Nashville: Broadman Press, 1984.

Hurley, James B. *Men and Women in Biblical Perspective.* Grand Rapids: Zondervan, 1981.

Kessler, Jay, ed. *Parents and Teenagers.* Wheaton, Ill.: Victor Books, 1984.

Kessler, Jay; Beers, Ron; and Neff, LaVonne; eds. *Parents and Children.* Wheaton, Ill.: Victor Books, 1986.

Lewis, J., and Beavers, R., et al. *No Single Thread: Psychological Health in Family Systems.* New York: Brunner-Mazel, 1976.

MacArthur, John, Jr. *The Family.* Chicago: Moody Press, 1982.

Mace, David R., ed. *Prevention in Family Services: Approaches to Family Wellness.* Beverly Hills, Calif.: Sage Publications, 1983.

Martin, Grant. *Please Don't Hurt Me.* Wheaton, Ill.: Victor Books, 1987.

Maston, T. B., and Tillman, William M., Jr. *The Bible and Family Relations.* Nashville: Broadman Press, 1983.

McDowell, Josh, and Lewis, Paul. *Givers, Takers, and Other Kinds of Lovers.* Wheaton, Ill.: Tyndale House, 1980.

Money, Royce. *Building Stronger Families.* Wheaton, Ill.: Victor Books, 1984.

Narramore, Bruce. *Parenting with Love and Limits.* Grand Rapids: Zondervan, 1979.

National Council on Family Relations. "A Special Issue: Family Life Education," *Family Relations: Journal of Applied Family and Child Studies,* October 1981, Volume 30, Number 4.

Navigators. *Parents and Children.* Colorado Springs: Navpress, 1980.

Ozment, Steven. *When Fathers Ruled: Family Life in Reformation Europe.* Cambridge, Mass.: Harvard University Press, 1983.

Rekers, George A., ed. *Family Building: Six Qualities of a Strong Family.* Ventura, Calif.: Regal Books, 1985.

Research and Forecasts, Inc. *The Connecticut Mutual Life Report on American Values in the Eighties.* Hartford: Connecticut Mutual Life Insurance Company, 1981.

Schaeffer, Edith. *What Is a Family?* Old Tappan, N.J.: Fleming H. Revell, 1975.

Sell, Charles M. *Family Ministry: The Enrichment of Family Life Through the Church.* Grand Rapids: Zondervan, 1981.

Stinnett, Nick, and DeFrain, John. *Secrets of a Strong Family.* Boston: Little, Brown and Co., 1985.

Stinnett, Nick, et al., eds. *Building Family Strengths: Blueprints for Action.* Lincoln: University of Nebraska Press, 1979.

Strommen, Merton P., and Strommen, A. Irene. *Five Cries of Parents.* San Francisco: Harper and Row, 1985.

Sussman, Marvin B., and Steinmetz, Suzanne K., eds. *Handbook of Marriage and the Family.* New York: Plenum, 1986.

Swihart, Judson J. *How to Treat Your Family as Well as You Treat Your Friends.* Ventura, Calif.: Regal Books, 1982.

Vaughan, Victor C., III, and Brazelton, T. Berry, eds. *The Family—Can It Be Saved?* Chicago: Yearbook Medical Publishers, Inc., 1976.

Ward, Ted. *Values Begin at Home.* Wheaton, Ill.: Victor Books, 1979.

Yankelovich, Daniel. *New Rules: Searching for Self-Fulfillment in a World Turned Upside Down.* New York: Random House, 1981.

NOTES

Introduction

1. I was invited to provide both oral and written expert testimony to this U.S. Senate Subcommittee on March 22, 1983. The transcript of my testimony on the topic, "Father Absence in Broken Families: The Effects on Children's Development," is published in "An Oversight on the Breakdown of the Traditional Family Unit," in *Hearings Before the Subcommittee on Family and Human Services, Committee on Labor and Human Resources, United States Senate*. Washington, D.C.: U.S. Government Printing Office, 1983, pp. 131–75. This same publication, the size of a small book, contains the oral and written testimony of Dr. George Gallup and other experts who were invited to submit information at that same set of hearings.

2. Stephen Quackenbos, Gayle Privette, and Bonnell Klentz, "Psychotherapy: Sacred or Secular?" *Journal of Counseling and Development* 63 (January 1985): 290–93.

3. Paul C. Glick, "Children From One-Parent Families: Recent Data and Projections," paper based on U.S. Bureau of the Census data and presented at the Special Institute on Critical Issues in Education, sponsored by the Charles F. Kettering Foundation, held at the American University, Washington, D.C., June 22, 1981. See also the Ford Foundation working paper entitled *Woman, Children, and*

Poverty in America, Ford Foundation, Office of Reports, 320 East 43 Street, New York, New York 10017, January 1985. See also "Children Captivate Congress," *U.S. News and World Report*, May 11, 1987, p. 28.

4. Armand M. Nicholi, Jr., M.D., "Commitment to Family," in *Family Building: Six Qualities of a Strong Family*, ed. George Rekers (Ventura, Calif.: Regal Books, 1985), 62.

5. Donald E. Wildmon, *The Home Invaders* (Wheaton, Ill.: Victor Books, 1985); T. B. Maston and W. M. Tillman, Jr., *The Bible and Family Relations* (Nashville: Broadman Press, 1983), 7–9.

Chapter 1 The Need for Family Counseling

1. Nicholi, "Commitment to Family," 51–52.

2. Paul C. Glick, "Children from One-Parent Families"; also, the Ford Foundation, *Woman, Children, and Poverty in America*; "Children Captivate Congress," *U.S. News and World Report*.

3. Ford Foundation, *Woman, Children, and Poverty in America*.

4. Nick Stinnett, "Six Qualities That Make Families Strong," in *Family Building*, ed. George Rekers, 36; William R. Garrett, *Seasons of Marriage and Family Life* (New York: Holt, Rinehart and Winston, 1982), 327–30.

5. Paul C. Glick, "Children from One-Parent Families"; Linette Long, *The Handbook for Latchkey Children and Their Parents* (Arbor House, 1983); Dean Merrill, "After-School Orphans," *Christianity Today*, August 10, 1984, 25–29.

6. Nicholi, "Commitment to Family," 53.

7. Ibid.

8. William H. Masters, Virginia E. Johnson, and Robert C. Kolodny, *Human Sexuality* (Boston: Little, Brown and Company, 1982), 350–52; *Attorney General's Commission on Pornography: Final Report* (Washington, D.C.: U.S. Department of Justice, July 1986), 595–617; David Alexander Scott, *Pornography: Its Effects on the Family, Community and Culture* (Washington, D.C.: Child and Family Protection Institute, 1985), 16–20; V. Fisher and D. Weisberg, *Juvenile Prostitution* (Lexington, Mass.: Lexington Books, 1983); M. Janus, V. Scanlon, and V. Prince, "Youth Prostitution," in *Child Pornography and Sex Rings*, ed. A. Burgess (Lexington, Mass.: Lexington Books, 1984), 127–46.

9. C. M. Hetherington, M. Cox, and R. Cox, "The Development of Children in Mother-Headed Families," in *The American*

Family: Dying or Developing, ed. D. Reiss (New York: Plenum, 1979), 117–45.

10. Shasta L. Mead and George A. Rekers, "The Role of the Father in Normal Psychosexual Development," *Psychological Reports* 45 (1979): 923–31; B. Berg and R. Kelly, "The Measure of Self-Esteem of Children from Broken, Rejected, and Accepted Families," *Journal of Divorce* 2 (1979): 363–69; H. Biller, "The Father and Personality Development: Paternal Deprivation and Sex-Role Development," in *The Role of the Father in Child Development,* ed. M. E. Lamb (New York: John Wiley, 1976), 89–156; J. S. Brook, M. Whiteman, and A. S. Gordon, "Father Absence, Perceived Family Characteristics and Stage of Drug Use in Adolescence," *British Journal of Development Psychology* 3 (1985): 87–94; K. Cobell and W. Turnbull, "The Long-Term Effects of Father Absence in Childhood on Male University Students' Sex-Role Identity and Personal Adjustment," *Journal of Genetic Psychology* 141 (1982): 271–76; George A. Rekers, "Children Need Involved Fathers: How the Father's Involvement in the Family Uniquely Contributes to the Social, Psychological, and Moral Development and Well-Being of Children and Adolescents," presented at the Capital Hill hearing, The National Family Strengths Project, U.S. House of Representatives, Labor Office Building, June 12, 1986; L. Yablonsky, *Fathers and Sons* (New York: Simon and Schuster, 1982); George A. Rekers, "Fathers at Home: Why the Intact Family Is Important to Children and the Nation," *Persuasion at Work* 9 (April 1986): 1–7.

11. Gerald P. Regier, ed., *Cultural Trends and the American Family* (Washington, D.C.: Family Research Council, 1986), 9–10; Peter Uhlenberg and David Eggebeen, "The Declining Well-Being of American Adolescents," *The Public Interest* 82 (Winter 1986): 25–38.

12. Uhlenberg and Eggebeen, "Declining Well-Being," 13.

13. Daniel Yankelovich, *New Rules: Searching for Self-Fulfillment in a World Turned Upside Down* (New York: Random House, 1981).

14. Francis A. Schaeffer and C. Everett Koop, *Whatever Happened to the Human Race?* (Old Tappan, N.J.: Fleming H. Revell, 1979).

15. George A. Rekers and Gerald P. Regier, *The Christian World View of the Family* (Mountainview, Calif.: The Coalition on Revival, 1986); Maston and Tillman, *The Bible and Family Relations.*

16. In the Bible, the terms "clan," "tribe," and "nation" are used for these larger family branches. See the varying uses in Scripture of the Hebrew word *mishpahah* (for example, Judges 18:2; Amos 3:1).

17. Rekers and Regier, *The Christian World View of the Family.*

Chapter 2 Detecting the Underlying Problems

1. W. Kempler, *Principles of Gestalt Family Therapy* (Oslo: Trykkeri, 1973).

2. Virginia Satir, *Conjoint Family Therapy* (Palo Alto, Calif.: Science and Behavior Books, 1967).

3. J. E. Bell, *Family Therapy* (New York: Jason Aronson, 1975).

4. J. Haley, *Problem-Solving Therapy* (San Francisco: Jossey-Bass, 1976).

5. W. Kempler, "Experiential Psychotherapy with Families," *Family Process* 7 (1968): 88–89; Kempler, *Gestalt Family Therapy.*

6. Satir, *Conjoint Family Therapy.*

7. G. H. Zuk, *Family Therapy: A Triadic-Based Approach* (New York: Human Sciences Press, 1971).

8. J. A. Larsen, "Family Diagram," in *Baker Encyclopedia of Psychology,* ed. David G. Benner (Grand Rapids: Baker Book House, 1985), 395.

9. This outline of questions incorporates many of the factors presented in an outline for family diagnosis in George Thorman, *Family Therapy: A Handbook* (Los Angeles: Western Psychological Services, 1975).

10. V. L. Shepperson, "Family Systems Theory," in *Baker Encyclopedia of Psychology,* ed. David G. Benner, 399–402.

11. The idea of "family rules" was first conceptualized by D. D. Jackson, "Family Rules: Marital Quid Pro Quo," *Archives of General Psychiatry* 12 (1965): 589–94.

12. Subsystem boundaries in a family have been conceptualized by Salvador Minuchin, *Families and Family Therapy* (Cambridge, Mass.: Harvard University Press, 1974).

13. Ibid.

14. I am indebted to Dr. Judson J. Swihart, president of the International Family Center, Logos Research Institute, Inc., in Manhattan, Kansas, for this analogy. In addition to being a very competent and experienced family counselor, Judd lives on a farm and he is given to making earthy analogies to family counseling situations, as in this analogy using a common farm commodity—peas.

15. S. Minuchin, B. L. Rosman, and L. Baker, *Psychosomatic Families* (Cambridge, Mass.: Harvard University Press, 1978).

16. Minuchin, *Families and Family Therapy.*

17. Irene Goldenberg and Herbert Goldenberg, *Family Therapy: An Overview* (Monterey, Calif.: Brooks/Cole Publishing Company, 1980), 20–22; George Thorman, *Family Therapy: A Handbook,*

9–11; S. Richard Sauber, Luciano L'Abate, and Gerald R. Weeks, *Family Therapy: Basic Concepts and Terms* (Rockville, Md.: Aspen, 1985), 69.

18. Shasta Mead and George A. Rekers, "The Role of the Father in Normal Psychosexual Development," 923–31; George A. Rekers, "Fathers at Home: Why the Intact Family Is Important to Children and the Nation."

19. Stephen A. Grunlan, *Marriage and the Family: A Christian Perspective* (Grand Rapids: Academie Books, Zondervan, 1984), 251–78; Maston and Tillman, *The Bible and Family Relations*.

20. James B. Hurley, *Man and Woman in Biblical Perspective* (Grand Rapids: Zondervan, 1981).

21. Goldenberg and Goldenberg, *Family Therapy: An Overview*, 25.

22. Bell, *Family Therapy*; Thorman, *Family Therapy: A Handbook*, 11.

23. Goldenberg and Goldenberg, *Family Therapy: An Overview*, 63–65.

24. Portions of this outline were suggested by and adapted from George Thorman, *Family Therapy: A Handbook*, 8–9.

25. See discussion by Goldenberg and Goldenberg, *Family Therapy: An Overview*, 138.

26. See review by L. R. Robinson, "Basic Concepts in Family Therapy: A Differential Comparison with Individual Treatment," *American Journal of Psychiatry* 132 (1975): 1045–1054.

27. D. Quinton and M. Redder, "Family Pathology and Child Psychiatric Disorder: A Four-Year Prospective Study," in *Longitudinal Studies in Child Psychology and Psychiatry: Practical Lessons from Research Experience*, ed. A. R. Nicol (Chichester, England: John Wiley and Sons, 1985), 91–134.

28. Minuchin, *Families and Family Therapy*.

29. A. R. Nicol, ed., *Longitudinal Studies*.

30. See articles in *Baker Encyclopedia of Psychology*, ed. David G. Benner (Grand Rapids: Baker Book House, 1985).

31. Stinnett, "Six Qualities That Make Families Strong," 41–42.

32. G. Bateson, D. Jackson, J. Haley, and J. Weakland, "Toward a Theory of Schizophrenia," *Behavioral Science* 1 (1956): 251–64; Goldenberg and Goldenberg, *Family Therapy: An Overview*, 86–88.

33. T. Lidz. S. Fleck, and A. Cornelison, *Schizophrenia and the Family* (New York: International University's Press, 1965); Sauber, L'Abate, and Weeks, *Family Therapy: Basic Concepts and Terms*, 122.

34. Portions of this checklist were suggested by and adapted from a list of diagnostic questions by George Thorman, *Family Therapy: A Handbook*, 7–8.

35. Ibid., 9–15.

36. Ibid.

37. M. Bowen, "A Family Concept of Schizophrenia," in *The Etiology of Schizophrenia*, ed. D. D. Jackson (New York: Basic Books, 1960).

38. M. Bowen, *Family Therapy in Clinical Practice* (New York: Jason Aronson, 1978).

39. L. Wynne, "The Study of Intrafamilial Alignments and Splits in Exploring Family Therapy," in *Exploring the Base for Family Therapy*, ed. N. Ackerman et al. (New York: Family Service Association of America, 1961): 95–115.

40. What I have referred to as "surface peace" is known technically in family therapy literature as "pseudo-mutuality," which is a term used by Wynne, "Intrafamilial Alignments and Splits."

41. George A. Rekers and Judson Swihart, *Making Up the Difference* (Grand Rapids: Baker Book House, 1984.)

42. Ibid.

Chapter 3 Biblical Perspectives for Goal Setting

1. Garry Willis, "What Religious Revival?" *Psychology Today*, April, 1978.

2. John Crothers Pollock et al., *The Connecticut Mutual Life Report on American Values in the '80s: The Impact of Belief* (Hartford: Connecticut Mutual Life Insurance Company, 1981). The research for this study was conducted by Research and Forecast, Inc. of New York, N.Y.

3. Ibid., 50.

4. Ibid., 127.

5. Ibid., 125.

6. Ibid., 135.

7. Ibid.

8. *The Unchurched American* (Princeton, N.J.: Princeton Religion Research Center and the Gallup Organization, 1978).

9. J. Robertson McQuilkin, *The Behavioral Sciences Under the Authority of Scripture* (Columbia, S.C.: Columbia Bible College and Seminary, 1976).

10. For further detail on this and other summaries of a biblical perspective on family life, see Rekers and Regier, eds., *The Christian World View of the Family*. A number of the principles in this publication have been paraphrased and adapted to the unique setting of Christian family counseling in the remaining sections of this chapter.

Chapter 4 Goals of Family Counseling

1. Gary R. Collins, "How Expressing Appreciation in Families Can Help Prevent Problems," in *Family Building: Six Qualities of a Strong Family*, ed. George Rekers.
2. Collins, "Expressing Appreciation," 286.
3. Hurley, *Man and Woman in Biblical Perspective*.
4. Charles G. Ward, *The Billy Graham Christian Workers' Handbook: A Layman's Guide for Soulwinning and Personal Counseling* (Minneapolis: Worldwide Publications, 1984), 5–13.

Chapter 5 Wellness and Family Counseling

1. Daniel Coats, "Commitment to Families by National Leaders," in *Family Building*, ed. George Rekers, 170.
2. Stinnett, "Six Qualities That Make Families Strong," 36.
3. Ibid., 37.
4. Elizabeth A. Morgan, *Pioneer Research on Strong, Healthy Families* (Washington, D.C.: Family Research Council, 1987); Laurence R. Barnhill, "Healthy Family Systems," *The Family Coordinator* 28 (January 1979): 94–100; Dolores Curran, *Traits of a Healthy Family* (Minneapolis: Winston Press, 1983); Robert B. Hill, *The Strengths of Black Families* (New York: Emerson Hall Publishers, 1971); Jerry M. Lewis, W. Robert Beavers, John Gossett, and Virginia Osten Phillips, *No Single Thread: Psychological Health in Family Systems* (New York: Brunner-Mazel, 1976); David H. Olson and Hamilton I. McCubbin and associates, *Families: What Makes Them Work?* (Beverly Hills: Sage Publications, 1983); Herbert A. Otto, "The Personal and Family Strength Research Projects: Some Implications for the Therapist," *Mental Hygiene* 48 (1964): 439–50; Nick Stinnett, Greg Sanders, John DeFrain, and Anne Parkhurst, "The Nationwide Study of Families Who Perceive Themselves as Strong," *Family Perspective* 16 (Winter 1982): 15–22.

5. Nick Stinnett and John DeFrain, *Secrets of Strong Families* (Boston: Little, Brown and Company, 1985).

6. Stinnett, "Six Qualities That Make Families Strong," 39.

7. Nicholi, "Commitment to Family," 53.

8. Stinnett, "Six Qualities That Make Families Strong," 39.

9. Nicholi, "Commitment to Family," 53.

10. Ibid.

11. Judson J. Swihart, "Teaching Communication Skills to Families," in *Family Building,* ed. George Rekers, 293.

12. Grace H. Ketterman, "Good Family Communication," in *Family Building,* ed. George Rekers, 107–9.

13. Ibid., 110–14.

14. Sherwood Eliot Wirt and Kersten Beckstrom, *Living Quotations for Christians* (New York: Harper and Row, 1974), 9.

15. J. Allan Petersen, "Expressing Appreciation," in *Family Building,* ed. George Rekers, 92.

16. Elizabeth A. Morgan, *Pioneer Research on Strong, Healthy Families*; David B. Larson, "Religious Involvement: Its Association with Marital Status, Marital Well-Being and Mortality," in *Family Building,* ed. George Rekers, 121–47.

17. Stinnett, "Six Qualities That Make Families Strong," 43–44.

18. Larson, "Religious Involvement," 137–41.

19. Francis A. Schaeffer, *How Should We, Then, Live?* (Old Tappan, N.J.: Fleming H. Revell Company, 1976).

20. See *The Christian Counselor's Handbook* (Wheaton, Ill.: Tyndale House Publishers, 1987), 95–108.

21. Gary R. Collins, *How to Be a People Helper* (Ventura, Calif.: Regal Books, 1976).

22. Win Arn, "Can We Close the Back Door? Overcoming the High Dropout Rates of Most Evangelistic Efforts," *Pastoral Renewal* 10 (February 1986): 102, 117–20.

23. Francis A. Schaeffer, *The Complete Works of Francis A. Schaeffer—A Christian World View. Vol. 1, A Christian View of Philosophy and Culture* (Westchester, Ill.: Crossway Books, 1982), 135.

24. Ibid., 133–34.

25. Ibid., 137, 138.

26. Ibid., 140.

27. Warren R. Schumm, "Beyond Relationship Characteristics of Strong Families: Constructing a Model of Family Strengths," *Family Perspective* 19 (1, 1985): 1–9.

28. William P. Wilson, "Problem-Solving in Crises," in *Family Building,* ed. George Rekers, 149–64.

Chapter 6 Approaches to Family Counseling

1. Thorman, *Family Therapy: A Handbook*, 15–19. The case studies beginning on pages 126 and 137 were adapted, expanded, and paraphrased from Thorman's handbook.

2. Raymond M. Bergner, "Emotions: A Conceptual Formulation and Its Clinical Implications," in *Advances in Descriptive Psychology*, ed. Keith E. Davis and Raymond M. Bergner (New York: JAI Press, 1983), 3: 209–27.

3. Curran, *Traits of a Healthy Family*.

4. I am indebted to a recorded lecture by the late Dr. Francis Schaeffer which I heard while studying at the L'Abri Fellowship Foundation (Huemoz, Switzerland) in June and July 1982, for this theological insight.

5. See Thorman, *Family Therapy: A Handbook*, 18–19.

6. Ibid.

7. Collins, "Expressing Appreciation," 281–92.

8. See chapter 3.

Chapter 7 Methods of Family Counseling

1. Goldenberg and Goldenberg, *Family Therapy: An Overview*, 107–29, 165–200.

2. A. S. Gurman and D. P. Kniskern, "Family Therapy Outcome Research: Knowns and Unknowns," in *Handbook of Family Therapy*, ed. A. S. Gurman and D. P. Kniskern (New York: Brunner-Mazel, 1981); D. H. Olson, C. S. Russell, and D. S. Sprenkle, "Marital and Family Therapy: A Decade Review," *Journal of Marriage and the Family* 42 (1980): 973–93; C. S. Russell, D. H. Olson, D. S. Sprenkle, and R. B. Atilano, "From Family Symptom to Family Systems: Review of Family Therapy Research," *American Journal of Family Therapy* 11 (1983): 3–14.

3. H. A. Evans, L. Chagoya, and V. Rakoff, "Decision-Making as to the Choice of Family Therapy in an Adolescent In-Patient Setting," *Family Process* 10 (1971): 97–110; Minuchin, Rosman, and Baker, *Psychosomatic Families*; M. D. Stanton, T. C. Todd, and associates, *The Family Therapy of Drug Abuse and Addiction* (New York: Guilford Press, 1981); J. Weakland, R. Fisch, P. Watzlawick, and A. Bodin, "Brief Therapy: Focused Problem Resolution," *Family Process* 13 (1974): 141–68; D. Beal and T. Duckro, "Family Counseling as an Alternative to Legal Action for the Juvenile

Status Offender," *Journal of Marriage and Family Counseling* 3 (1977): 77–81.

4. M. Rohrbaugh, "Q-Sort Comparison of the Structural, Strategic and Systemic Family Therapies" (Paper presented at the American Psychological Association annual meeting, Washington, D.C., 1982).

5. William H. Quinn and Bernard Davison, "Prevalence of Family Therapy Models: A Research Note," *Journal of Marital and Family Therapy* 10 (1984): 393–98.

6. Adapted from C. S. Russell, R. B. Atilano, S. A. Anderson, A. P. Gurich, and L. P. Bergen, "Intervention Strategies: Predicting Family Therapy Outcome," *Journal of Marital and Family Therapy* 10 (1984): 241–51.

7. Thorman, *Family Therapy: A Handbook*, 19.

8. Sauber, L'Abate, and Weeks, *Family Therapy: Basic Concepts and Terms*, 146.

9. Thorman, *Family Therapy: A Handbook*, 19.

10. Also adapted from Russell, Atilano, Anderson, Jurich, and Bergen, "Intervention Strategies."

11. Ibid., 249.

12. Also adapted from Russell, Atilano, Anderson, Jurich, and Bergen, "Intervention Strategies." See also James C. Coyne, "Toward a Theory of Frames and Reframing: The Social Nature of Frames," *Journal of Marital and Family Therapy* 11 (1985): 337–44.

13. Russell, Atilano, Anderson, Gurich, and Bergen, 249.

14. See Thorman, *Family Therapy: A Handbook*, 19–20.

15. Ibid.

16. Ibid.

17. Adapted from Russell, Atilano, Anderson, Gurich, and Bergen, "Intervention Strategies." For detail regarding strategies for changing specific behavior patterns, see Gerald R. Patterson, *Families: Applications of Social Learning to Family Life*, rev. ed. (Champaign, Ill.: Research Press, 1978).

18. Ibid.

Chapter 8 Challenges in Family Counseling

1. This case study was adapted and paraphrased from H. Goldenberg, *Abnormal Psychology, A Social/Community Approach* (Monterey, Calif.: Brooks/Cole Publishing Company, 1977), 350–51.

INDEX

George A. Rekers

George A. Rekers, Ph.D. in psychology from the University of California at Los Angeles, is licensed both as a marriage/family/child counselor and as a clinical psychologist, holding the Diplomate in Clinical Psychology from the American Board of Professional Psychology. Dr. Rekers is currently a full-time professor in the medical school of a major state university, where he also pursues a part-time clinical practice in the teaching hospital. Previously, he was professor and chairman of the Marriage and Family Therapy Unit and a Department Head at Kansas State University and a visiting scholar at Harvard University. Dr. Rekers recently served as a visiting professor in family counseling at the Tyndale Theological Seminary in the Netherlands, and at the Columbia Biblical Seminary.

Having received over half a million dollars in grants for his clinical research, Professor Rekers has authored and edited books and over sixty academic articles on counseling families of disturbed children. He recently provided expert testimony on family issues before the U.S. Senate, the U.S. House of Representatives, a Task Force of the U.S. Attorney General, and the staff of the White House Domestic Policy Council. Dr. Rekers was the founding chairman of the Family Research Council and remains on its board. He and his wife, Sharon, reside in Columbia, South Carolina with their five sons: Steven, Andrew, Matthew, Timothy, and Mark.